Discovering ORFF

A Curriculum for Music Teachers

Jane Frazee

with

Kent Kreuter

SCHOTT

Mainz · London · New York · Tokyo

This book is dedicated to Aleda Christensen
and to Betsy and David Kreuter

ISBN 0 930448 99 5

Designed by Geoffrey Wadsley
Typeset and printed by
Ian Allan Printing Limited
Coombelands House, Coombelands Lane,
Addlestone, Surrey, England.

Contents

Acknowledgements

This book commemorates the encouragement and example of my many friends and teachers over the years. This public acknowledgement is intended to express my private gratitude for their inestimable contributions to my life and work.

My heartfelt thanks go to Druanne Sweetser, a first-grade teacher whose respect for children convinced me of the worthiness of the profession; James Frazee, who encouraged and supported my work with wit and patience for twenty years; Jack Johnson, Dean of Graduate and Continuing Studies at Hamline University, who has taken risks to promote my new music education programs; George Schumacher, Catherine Gately, and Wm E. Harris and the faculty and staff at St Paul Academy and Summit School who have provided the healthy climate necessary for my work with children; Hermann Regner, who by extending me many invitations to the Orff Institute gave testimony to the fact that this place, like the work it fosters, encourages diversity of thought; Richard Gill, who consistently inspires my appreciation for what Orff work can be when taught by an intelligent, articulate musician; Jos Wuytack, who was the first to stimulate my quest for sound pedagogical foundations for Orff activities and whose composition teaching has given me a voice for my own music; Nancy Miller, whose music-and-movement work consistently demonstrates her affection and respect for children; Jacobeth Postl, who for twenty-five years has challenged my ideas and provided well-timed encouragement; Mary Goetze, whose work is a constant reminder that art is the goal of the craft of music teaching; Arvida Steen, for whom music education is a labor of love — she has been my trusted, steadfast friend and colleague during these important years; Judy Bond, who has taught me that serenity and Orff teaching are not antithetical; the American Orff-Schulwerk Assocation, which has provided an invaluable forum to try out my ideas and to learn from others; my students – children and adults – who teach me every day; and my dear husband, Kent Kreuter, whose enthusiastic collaboration gave life to this book.

Preface

'Whenever I plant a tree, I never know how big it will be . . . Some trees stay small, others grow very tall. It all depends on the quality of the earth, sunshine and other factors that have to work together.' This was the answer given to me by Carl Orff in a radio interview I held with him in 1975 when I asked him if he knew or had any idea or expectation that his Schulwerk would be accepted by so many teachers throughout the world.

It would seem that the earth in many lands is really quite good and that much sunshine has contributed to growth. Consider the fact that since 1950 these are the published versions of Orff-Schulwerk: German, English, Swedish, Dutch, Latin-American, Portuguese, Japanese, Spanish, French, Welsh, Czechoslovakian, Chinese, Danish, Korean, Italian and an adaptation for the United States. Supplements and other editions have come from Greece, Brazil, Bolivia, Ghana and Estonia. In other countries the ideas of the Schulwerk or of using the instruments play a significant role. Since 1961 students from forty-eight different countries have studied at the Orff Institute of the Hochschule 'Mozarteum' in Salzburg.

This book describes the basic ideas of Orff-Schulwerk for the classroom in the United States. It states concretely how its media, pedagogy and theory must be interwoven in order to give whole classes and individual children musical competence. It also serves as a motivating source for teachers to set out on their own voyages of discovery to Orff-Schulwerk.

This book talks a lot about the Orff Schulwerk teacher. Thank goodness there is no such thing as a description of the typical teacher. There has never been any research to establish statistical facts which could very well result in a ridiculous statement like: 'The Orff teacher is someone between the ages of thirty-seven and forty, female, blond, eager to travel, and who plays a good game of chess!' A good teacher who works with the philosophy and materials from Orff-Schulwerk is full of ideas. He does not want to be a slave to a method which does not allow him the freedom to make pedagogical decisions in each separate teaching situation.

The teacher Carl Orff had in mind is an artistic being with good taste; sensitive, spontaneous and responsive. As a teacher one must pay close attention to observing children. He has both the quick and vocal children in view as well as the slower and quieter ones. He is protective, can stay in the background when necessary and lead the children to warm associations with partners, with instruments and with music itself. The Orff-Schulwerk teacher is moreover a human being . . . one who can be full of joy and also anger, who can be happy and also sad; a human being with strengths and weaknesses. To the children he is a dependable partner, a person who animates without being too demanding, who accepts the individual efforts of the children and is not afraid to let his own ideas and demands for good quality be expressed along with theirs. For these reasons there is no such thing as the 'Orff-Schulwerk teacher'. There are many Orff-Schulwerk teachers, and no two are alike. Each one alone has the right and the obligation to contribute his own background, his experiences in music and movement, his understanding of Orff's ideas.

If all is so open, what then are the specific requisites? There are basic principles for working with Orff-Schulwerk that are set forth in this book. There are musical skills and concepts that give directions and goals to teaching. Furthermore, common to all Orff-Schulwerk teachers throughout the world is the caring about coming closer to a clear insight into music and movement that gives each participant a basic, fundamental experience. It has to do with the encounters these responsible teachers create in music and dance . . . not with pieces of music and separate dances, but with music and dance as universal and at the same time very specific media of human expression. It also has to do with the artistic quality intended by Carl Orff and Gunild Keetman in all the adaptations of the Schulwerk. This transfer into other cultures and into present and future times is necessary.

Carl Orff and collaborators throughout the world have thought for many years about how the vision of such an education for so many children and young adults can be realized in a constantly changing world. This book represents a carefully considered and wise step toward the answer.

Hermann Regner
Director, *Orff-Schulwerk Zentrum*, Salzburg

(translated by Miriam Samuelson)

Introduction

Not long ago a visiting family brought their young daughter to my school music room. She seemed intrigued by the surroundings and was soon playing a xylophone. As we watched, she moved on to drums, then to cymbals and glockenspiels until at last she had made her way through them all. When she finished she ran to me and said, 'I have played every single instrument in this whole room and it's like magic.' My guest musician was a seven-year-old named Rebecca. She had never before been in an Orff classroom.

Most Orff teachers regularly witness such discoveries. In this particular case, the magic Rebecca spoke of lay not only in the instrumental sounds but in the fact that *she* could use those instruments to make such sounds. And therein lies one of the reasons why Orff pedagogy is so effective and such stories are so commonplace. The Orff approach combines the love of sound, love of music-making, and the need to be appreciated in such a way that children can participate in their own musical education and personal growth. Not only are their minds and imaginations stimulated but they are also urged to feel and to give musical expression to that feeling.

The ultimate aim of Orff's approach to music is the enrichment of students' lives through the development of their inherent musicality. That goal is hardly unique to Orff, in fact many other methods claim the same intent. However, what makes Orff's approach special is the way it develops the idea that the child learns musical behavior through behaving in musical ways: by creating, listening and performing.

As Orff originally developed his perspective in the 1920s, creating was of central importance. Teaching consisted of presenting musical problems with students expected to improvise their own solutions. The end result was a musically independent student.

Listening was also of prime importance because all music in an Orff program was created by groups. In order to contribute, students had to listen to the sounds of others. Skill at self-evaluation would also be impossible without this ability as would the talent to understand music one lacked the technical facility to perform.

The last fundamental premise of Orff's conception made much of performance. All students were to perform all the time, be it singing, moving, speaking or playing. So important was participation that Orff designed or adapted instruments that facilitated student contributions, whatever their level of ability.

The music that inspired this creating, listening and performing was also special. Since Orff was a German teaching German-speaking students he used the rhymes, proverbs and poetry of that language to teach the rhythms of that culture. Finding little German folk material in the pentatonic scale, he wrote his own, the better to help students improvise. And as Orff's approach spread to a wider world in the 1950s he urged others to use comparable material from their own cultures.

This book does not radically alter Orff's goals and practices. Instead, the following pages take up where Orff left off. Content with developing the main objectives, he did not provide the step-by-step process needed to implement his intentions. We now know that such concerns need to be addressed. Hence this book is for those of you who want detailed, practical assistance in how and why to use Orff techniques and materials in your classrooms. We have made an effort to outline goals and explore the best ways to achieve them, but the principal focus is on the arrangement of the curriculum in a logical sequence. Such a structure provides a reasonable progression from simple to more complex objectives not only from day to day but from year to year.

Since an emphasis on sequence is rare in Orff literature, perhaps a few words of explanation are in order. I have placed a major emphasis on sequence because in more than twenty years as a teacher of both children and teachers of children it is clear that this is the greatest need. To some, this sequential approach may seem the rankest heresy since structured learning does appear to be the enemy of improvisation, surely one of the most characteristic features of Orff pedagogy. But for those who read on it will soon become clear that these pages abound with opportunities for student creativity. Actually, the real issue is not the merit of improvisation but rather how best to provide students with the tools they need to improvise. Not only my experience but that of many other teachers, suggests that those tools are best acquired in a carefully planned curriculum that develops steadily over the years. From such learning will come the independent musicianship we all so deeply want for our students.

In order to provide detailed assistance, we have arranged the book as follows: after an introduction to the development of Orff-Schulwerk we turn, in Part One, to a discussion of the distinguishing features of this approach. Chapter Two introduces the activities children use in their music-making. The teaching procedure that structures those activities is taken up in Chapter Three while Chapter Four explains the vocabulary and accompaniment theory essential to the Orff teacher. Part Two applies these elements in a sequential curriculum designed for Grades One through Five. Especially important in each chapter is the inclusion of supporting activities designed to aid you in teaching the various skills and concepts.

This book does not claim to have the magic formula for teaching excellence. Even if these pages contained nothing but wisdom such insight would be useless without the committed teacher. Rather, this book has the more modest intent of trying to help channel energies and talents so that you and your students can more easily make music that delights the ear and enriches the mind.

1 · The Gift and the Challenge of Carl Orff

Carl Orff's great gift is to children. In essence that gift is a way of looking at music that deeply involves them in its creation, and thereby entails respect for their capabilities.[1]

Orff's challenge is to teachers. He requires of us the care and ingenuity to devise the methods that will, in the daily wear-and-tear of teaching, not crush but bring to flower the capabilities that can so deeply enrich the lives of young people. Orff paid teachers the great compliment of assuming that because they were musicians as well as pedagogues, they would find their own ways to the musical and human ends he sought.

That teachers have been eager to accept the challenge is borne out by the swift rise of Orff instruction in this and many other countries since World War Two. Actually, that burst of interest is just one of the latest examples of a process nearly as old as America itself — the borrowing and adapting of European musical ideas to American circumstances. Such influence goes back at least to Pestalozzi and his great American disciple Lowell Mason and we can see further examples of this interplay in the impact of Jacques-Dalcroze and Kodály in our own time.

All of these methods have posed problems for their American adherents but none more so than Orff. The reasons are rooted in the particular interplay of personality and historical circumstances that shaped and fostered his ideas. Among these ideas improvisation is fundamental and even the most cursory view of Orff's early life shows how important it was to him. Early on, he developed a marked distaste for performing any music but his own. By the age of ten (in 1905) he was creating stories as well. Soon he branched off into theater, creating puppet plays scored for, among other things, the kitchen stove. When he began publishing his music a few years later, the originality — if not the stove — was still in evidence.

This intolerance for musical convention drew him to reformers like Mary Wigman and, particularly, Dorothee Günther. These two remarkable women were revolutionizing dance in Germany, and Wigman was fast becoming the continental equivalent of Isadora Duncan. Out of this association, no doubt fuelled by the excitement born of much talk and collaboration, came the decision in 1923 to found the Güntherschule in Munich, a place where young, aspiring musicians could deepen and enrich their musical understanding through a synthesis of music and dance. It would be no ordinary school. For one thing, Orff wanted it free of 'the deficient or out-of-date musical activity that was customary in most gymnastic schools', as he put it.[2] For another, it would replace the old, shop-worn approaches with what Orff called 'elemental music'. By that he meant an improvised music shorn of centuries of convention; a music that was magical and spiritual and pure, played on the instruments of primitive peoples and using movement as a fundamental component. First and last, the Güntherschule was *not* where one went to reproduce the rights and wrongs of other people's music.

In some respects the Germany where Orff and his allies were dreaming their dreams could not have been a worse place to be. The legacies of World War One included much political and social unrest coupled with and fed by severe economic problems. And yet, perhaps in even more significant ways, Germany in the 1920s was the perfect place for creative men and women intent on changing a corner of cultural life. While the war had taken a tremendous toll it had also inadvertently undermined old ideas and old leadership. More than four years of unprecedented bloodshed had opened the door to those who championed the new. As the Bauhaus alone exemplifies, the atmosphere was rife with much creative energy and accomplishment. Hence Orff, innovative from almost his first day, now found himself quite unexpectedly in a social environment much more conducive to experimentation than he had any right to expect. Tragically, it was a time quickly passed.

Orff and his friends were equal to that fleeting opportunity. In September of 1924 the school opened and what Orff liked to call his 'new balancing act' began its educational adventure.[3] Part of the adventure lay in the search for alternatives to Western music. The quest for the primitive, so powerful a force in much turn-of-the-century art, was also strong in Orff. In his case it meant turning to Africa and Asia for the percussion instruments he needed to create adequately his elemental music. But the principal addition in the mid-twenties was Gunild Keetman. In her creativity and energy Orff found the help he needed to sustain the Schulwerk.[4]

By the end of the decade the experiment in improvising with novel instrumentation and movement could be judged a success. The work of Orff and his associates was opening new vistas in the professional training of a growing number of young adults as well as making a more modest contribution to the spread of modern dance. Ironically enough, there even seemed a chance that this educational protest of the twenties might become the educational orthodoxy of the thirties. However, the arrival of National Socialism in 1933 meant that Orff's friends in high educational places soon had no places at all, and with this shift in power went any hope of a broad institutionalization of Orff methodology.

Yet this disastrous decade did contain one brief moment that turned out to have far-reaching consequences for the spread of Orff's approach to music education. That moment came with the 1936 Olympic games, held in Berlin, when Orff was asked to help in the composition of music for the opening festivities. The end result was processional music and a group dance for thousands of young children. Ironically, the situation could not have been less Orff-like. Instead of small groups of children improvising their own melodies, there were thousands of children performing the music and movement prescribed by others. However, out of that Olympic experience arose an entirely new and more significant emphasis in Orff education.

The crucial metamorphosis began in 1948 when a German administrator,

Annemarie Schambeck, listened to a recording of the music those children had performed twelve years earlier in Berlin. She had never before heard such music played on such instruments. Would Orff consider composing simpler versions so that young children could also play, she asked? Orff accepted the challenge, realizing that this new audience required a somewhat different approach.

The major change was a new stress on singing. It now seemed that the natural starting-point for children should be the songs of children. As he noted years later, 'the recognition of this fact gave me the key for the new educational work'.[5] Much else in his approach to this younger audience remained as it had in the Güntherschule. There was no need to change the instrumentation since xylophones and glockenspiels were more suited to the child's music-making than pianos and violins. At most, some reduction in the size of the instruments would be sufficient. Movement and improvisation would continue to be of fundamental importance as would the basic goal of awakening children to music. Given modest resources and enlightened teachers, children would soon be making music for children.

Propitious circumstances gave Orff a chance to try out his ideas. Unlike the early thirties when support was lost, Orff now had friends in key positions, such as Annemarie Schambeck who saw to it from her position with Bavarian radio, that children throughout Bavaria heard and performed the new music composed by Orff. And it seemed to work. One critic offered this early appraisal:

> The numerous letters and essays, questions and stimuli that have been sent in during this last half year give credence to the high pedagogical value of this musical work. It lies in education for independence. If school children send in melodies they have written . . . it is not a question of unusual talent but of children who have been awakened, for whom the elemental originality of the Schulwerk way of making music has released in them musical powers, that, if their musical education remains solely reproductive, stay buried.[6]

Also in 1948 the influential Mozarteum came under the direction of an old ally Eberhard Preussner. Quickly Keetman and others were reproducing for young children the work done at the Günterschule. Demonstrations soon followed in Austrian colleges. Meanwhile, a new associate, Klaus Becker, was producing appropriately sized instruments for the younger players. By 1950 the *Music for Children* volumes began to appear providing invaluable instructional materials. Translations into other languages quickly followed as did demonstrations of Orff techniques to foreign educators. Expansion to a wider world was beginning. A culmination to these years of growth came in 1963 with the opening of a permanent Orff Institute in Salzburg. Only one hundred miles and thirty-nine years separated this second home from the first but in many ways the past seemed much further away.

This brief survey of the birth, death and rebirth of Orff's musical pedagogy should enable us to gain a deeper understanding of not only the gift and the challenge he left us but of why adapting Orff to America has been a major part of that challenge.

Probably the best way to get at the essence of his approach is to think of it as a pedagogy of suggestion. As we have seen, Orff was determined not only to create but to inspire others to create. Hence the openness to innovation was quite intentional. This had tremendous liberating possibilities. For teachers who felt bored and confined by the conventional rote of music education it meant freedom. For children it meant liberation from mechanical instruction plus a chance to participate in their own musical growth.

But in this very openness lay a problem. Part of the difficulty arose from the kind of student Orff first tried to educate. Those who came to the Günterschule in the 1920s were young adult musicians and dancers. Consequently there was no need to teach the basic vocabulary of music. For Orff it seemed much more important and certainly far more exciting to have students discover the elemental qualities of music. This was to be an education in revitalization, not in quarter notes.

The crucially important result of this blend of literate student and brilliant, self-taught teacher was that no one found it necessary to think through how to teach the basic vocabulary of music. In fact, the very success of the Günterschule confirmed this absence. In addition, that success very likely attracted those least interested in teaching the less dramatic dimensions of music. This orientation made no difference as long as students were taught that vocabulary by someone else. But such was not always to be the case. Paradoxically, what began as a method assuming knowledge of the basics had soon to teach those basics itself. In fact, in America there never has been a student body of the sort Orff originally taught; the only students of Orff in this country are the youngsters he never considered when making his original plans.

Orff began to confront this problem after World War Two. The result was as we might expect: much emphasis on participation but very little on vocabulary. When Orff and Keetman began publishing their *Music for Children* volumes in 1950 that approach was retained, as it was in the English translation which soon followed.

Now, over thirty years later, we can see that while that approach has much to recommend it there is still need for further development. It is well and good to urge that children be given a chance to create. However, there is a much greater chance that something will come of that hope if teachers are given guidelines in how to lead children to that objective.

In the best of all possible educational systems, teachers make themselves superfluous. Orff wanted that but for reasons we have seen he didn't set forth the steps to accomplish what he thought so important. It is the purpose of this book to provide those steps.

Part One:

THE ELEMENTS OF ORFF-SCHULWERK

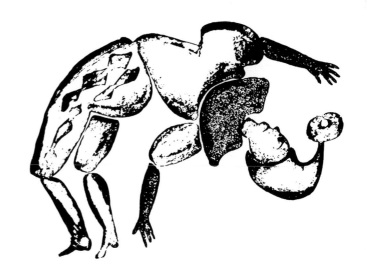

2 · Orff Media

The Orff approach to elementary music learning addresses every aspect of musical behavior: performing, creating, listening, and analyzing. But it is the variety of means by which these behaviors are cultivated that has created such delight in Orff classrooms. The original challenge to take a wider view of music education than the prevailing preoccupation with printed symbols came from Orff when he defined the ideal kind of music for children as, 'never music alone, but music connected with movement, dance, and speech – not to be listened to, meaningful only in active participation.'[1]

Orff teachers have responded to this challenge by offering their students a wide variety of participatory activities to foster musical growth including speech, movement, song, instruments, and listening.[2] Musical ideas are consistently explored through this array of active means in increasingly sophisticated ways. The activities may be used singly or in combination to involve the entire class in learning. Readiness, skill level, and activity preference will vary among the children; the Orff teacher respects these individual differences and so uses a variety of media to develop each child's maximum musical potential. For instance, a child who is not an able singer may master a given melodic motive on a bar instrument because visual reinforcement of the sound occurs when it is played. Skill mastery thus becomes possible for children who might not succeed in a one-dimensional approach. In fact, these activities provide avenues that lead to understanding and using *all* the elements of music.

Speech

The rhythm inherent in the child's native language is an important resource for Orff teachers. The rhymes, word-games, riddles, proverbs, and poems from the child's heritage offer unlimited possibilities for exploring musical elements. A few examples have been selected from the wide variety available to help illustrate some of the ways in which this is accomplished.

Spoken rhythms may be clapped and perhaps transferred to unpitched percussion instruments.

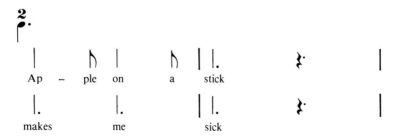

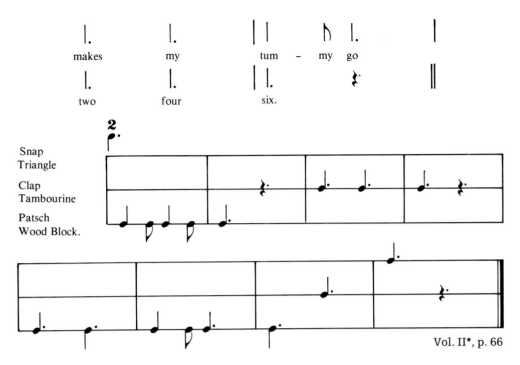

Rhymes are also particularly useful for meter and tempo exploration.

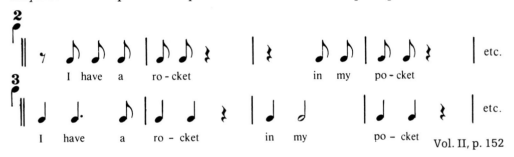

Two or more speech patterns may be combined to illustrate texture.

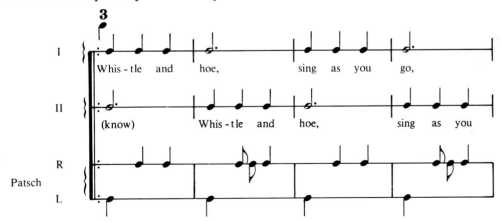

*All examples are drawn from *Music for Children*, American Edition, Volumes I-III, Schott Music Corp., 1977, 1980, 1982

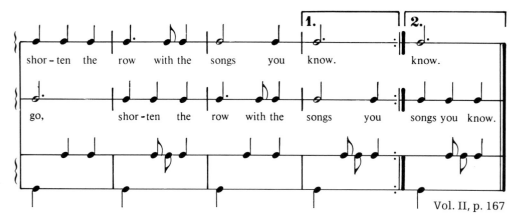

shor - ten   the   row   with the   songs   you   know.

1. know.

go,   shor -ten   the   row   with the   songs   you   songs you   know.

2.

Vol. II, p. 167

The use of vocal sounds (sometimes known as vocables) is a useful tone color teaching device.

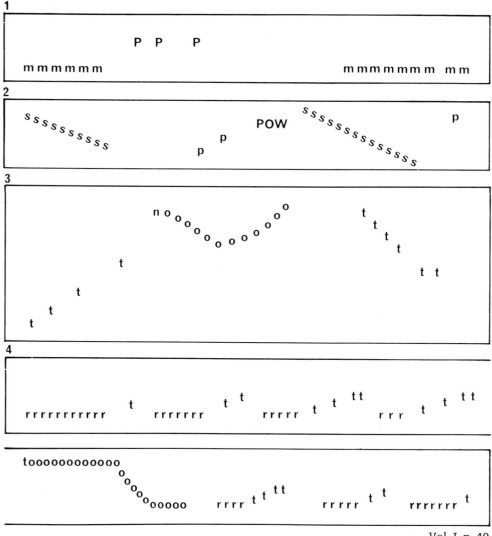

Vol. I, p. 49

Expressive elements such as dynamics and accent may be explored in speech work.

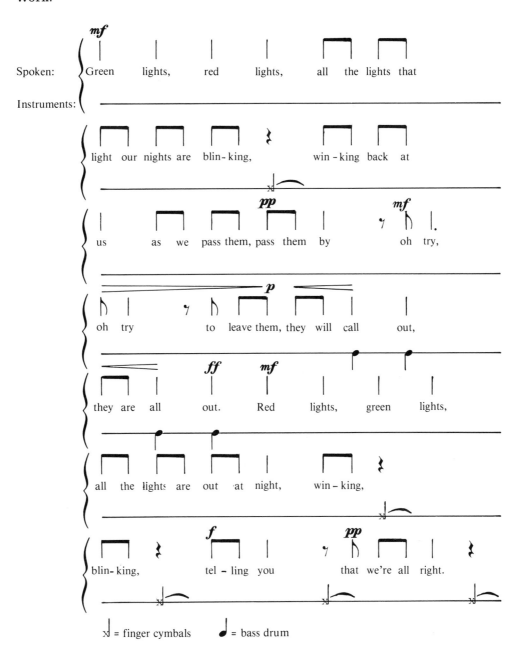

Spoken: Green lights, red lights, all the lights that
Instruments:

light our nights are blin- king, win - king back at

us as we pass them, pass them by oh try,

oh try to leave them, they will call out,

they are all out. Red lights, green lights,

all the lights are out at night, win - king,

blin- king, tel - ling you that we're all right.

♩ = finger cymbals ♩ = bass drum

Vol. II, p. 114

Speech activities are also well suited to the development of literacy and improvisation skills. Try asking your students to realize graphic or conventional scores with vocal sounds (vocables) or invite them to invent sound atmospheres for poems and stories.

17

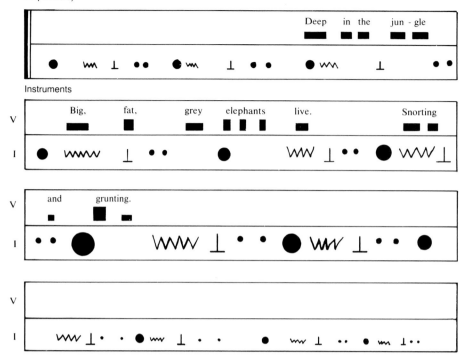

Voices (as deep as possible)

Deep in the jun-gle

Instruments

Big, fat, grey elephants live. Snorting

and grunting.

Key

● = bass–or deep hand-drum struck with soft mallet

w = guiro or reco-reco scraped with triangle beater

⊥ = large hanging cymbal struck with soft mallet and damped with one hand

● = wood block

The voice part should be spoken, with variations in pitch coming from the meaning of the words.

The piece may be varied as follows: The speed may be varied, either within the piece or from performance to performance. The sequence of instruments may be changed, or the conductor may indicate entrances by pointing, varying the sequence each time. However, dynamics and entrances in relation to the text should remain as marked (note especially wood block dynamics).

Vol. II, p. 54

Texture also is illustrated in body percussion, pitched, or unpitched percussion accompaniments to spoken texts.

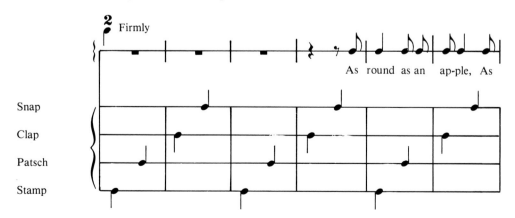

Firmly

As round as an ap-ple, As

Snap

Clap

Patsch

Stamp

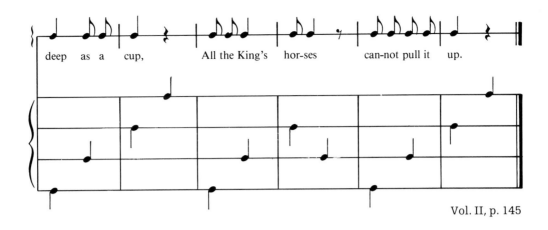

deep   as   a   cup,   All the King's   hor-ses   can-not pull it   up.

Vol. II, p. 145

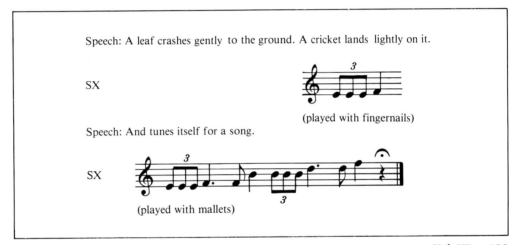

Speech: A leaf crashes gently to the ground. A cricket lands lightly on it.

SX

(played with fingernails)

Speech: And tunes itself for a song.

SX

(played with mallets)

Vol. III, p. 136

The close relationship of speech to singing is another important reason for including it in a total music program. In fact many young children often confuse the two. Comparisons between spoken and sung vocal color and range are helpful to children in the early stages of their vocal development. But whatever the level of competence, Orff teachers know that speech activities provide indispensable materials with which to build skill and sensitivity in the children they teach.

Movement

The importance of the kinesthetic aspect of musical performance is well understood by Orff teachers. They acknowledge physical response as the foundation upon which group music-making is laid, for when children can keep a collective beat and an established tempo they are ready for ensemble work. As is the case with the other activity areas, Orff teachers do not view movement study as an end in itself but as another means towards musical and emotional growth.

The presentation of movement activities follows a sequence closely related to that discussed in detail in Chapter Three: imitation, exploration, literacy, and improvisation. Because of this pedagogical overlap, music and movement reinforce one another quite naturally. Movement imitation involves following a leader simultaneously (mirror), at a specified time interval (echo), or at an interval which overlaps with the leader (canon). Exploration involves discovering the movement possibilities of the body. It can be related to exploring a variety of musical ideas using the elements of music. Structured sequences, patterned movement, dance forms, and choreography may be considered analogous to music literacy for both have a predetermined set of conditions for the performer to follow. Improvisation involves putting skills to work to invent new material and is of great importance in music-and-movement learning situations.

Movement is an indispensable aid for developing music skills and concepts. It can help the student assimilate such aspects of rhythm as pulse, pattern, meter, and tempo. Melodic direction and such qualities as dynamics and color can be expressed in movement; and movement illustrates texture, form, and dramatic situations in very concrete ways. All teachers know that children are typically in motion. Hence, Orff music education welcomes the possibilities for learning through the body as well as the brain because it is truly a child-centered approach.

Song

Orff teachers agree that the voice is the primary melody instrument. Skill in singing must be so carefully developed that children learn to respect their voices as they would a violin, recorder, or any other instrument they might study. Because it is so readily accessible, teachers tend to treat the voice more casually than other instruments played by children. It is important that this inequality of emphasis be righted; children must be taught basic tone-production and intonation in the early years of school.

Singing is the most immediate medium for exploring the relationship of one pitch to another. Melodic intervals are introduced in a careful sequence until the full pentatonic scale is assimilated. The introduction of diatonic major and minor is delayed until the upper elementary levels. Children are expected to be fully literate at each stage; they read, write, sing, and play all the intervals they know from notation.

In addition to melody learning, singing is an invaluable resource for studying other musical elements. Song rhythms are isolated, meter and tempo practiced, and texture explored. Counterpoint is introduced through rounds and canons and through vocal ostinati and counter-melodies which are sung simultaneously with the melody. Songs with simple harmonic changes can be accompanied by singing chord roots or by vocal chording. Songs also provide an abundance of material for teaching form, dynamics, and tone color. Folk songs offer short illustrative examples of sectional forms and contain smaller units of form such as motive and phrase.

Vocal improvisation is a good test of interval security and it offers students the opportunity to create original material within a specified context. If begun in the earliest stages with only two notes and in a helpful classroom atmosphere children will be willing to contribute original melodies in familiar tonal contexts at all stages of development.

Instruments

We all know that children are fascinated by sound. In fact, few can resist the opportunity to experiment with the wide variety of colors provided by Orff instruments. In an Orff ensemble your students will learn to listen, to appreciate, and to help one another in collective musical endeavors. Sound realizations for poems or stories, melodic accompaniments, and instrumental pieces are just a few of the many group music-making activities facilitated by classroom instruments.

In addition to providing an ideal medium for texture and color exploration, Orff instruments support young voices with aural and visual reinforcement of pitch relationships. Rhythmic patterns or phrases can be performed on contrasting unpitched percussion instruments, several complementary phrases can be layered to create a rhythmic or melodic composition. Formal construction can be highlighted by such instrumental colors as a B section for metal instruments contrasted with an A section performed by woods. These are just a few of the ways in which Orff instruments provide an invaluable means of exploring all of the elements of music.

Because of pitch and rhythm precision not typical of the voice, instruments also provide an ideal medium for improvisation. Your students might be challenged to develop contrasting sections for small forms, to add original rhythmic phrases to an ensemble piece, to make up melodies for texts, and to create background color for verses and stories. When they are secure in their environment and with their own skills, children are willing to take the kinds of risks which improvisation demands. The entire learning process offers no greater reward than the recognition by a child's peers of his or her unique and important creation.

(i) Voice and Body
Let us begin by exploring the instruments that children carry with them. The voice may be used for sound effects (vocables) as well as for singing.

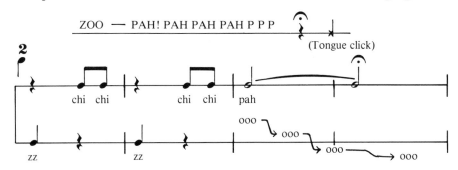

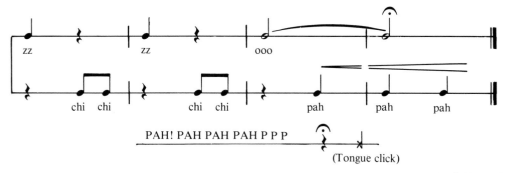

Vol. II, p. 73

The body itself provides a number of sound possibilities. Orff teachers typically use stepping, thigh-patting (called 'patschen' in many books), slapping, and finger-snapping for sound gesture compositions.

Vol. II, p. 65

(ii) Unpitched Percussion

Many kinds of high-quality unpitched percussion instruments are available for use in schools. These instruments are divided by sound quality into four categories: wood, metal, rattles and scrapers, and skin. For orchestration purposes unpitched instruments are ordinarily arranged on a score according to their ranges.

> metal: triangle, finger cymbal, cowbell, etc
> wood (including scraped): woodblock, claves, guiro, etc
> membranes: hand drums, bongo, etc
> large percussion: timpani, gong, hanging cymbal, etc.

The transfer from body percussion (or sound gestures) to unpitched instruments is a simple process. Finger-snaps become metal sounds, claps change to wood, pats to membranes, and steps to large percussion instruments. Transfer makes it possible for an entire class to learn a rhythmic composition in several parts before it is performed on percussion instruments.

A. Sound Gestures

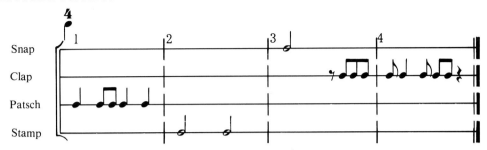

B. Non-Pitched Percussion   (Separate player for each instrument)

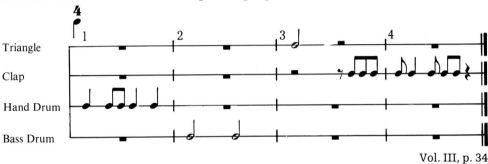

Vol. III, p. 34

(iii) Bar Instruments

Orff gave his name to a collection of melodic percussion bar instruments which he developed in the 1920s. It is perhaps this association which leads teachers unfamiliar with the variety of media used in this approach to view Orff-Schulwerk as an instrumental method for music teaching. Although the instruments are only one avenue to musicianship development, they are certainly one of the features which set this approach apart from traditional pedagogical methods.

The bar instruments put a wide range of register and resonance possibilities into the hands of relatively untrained players. (See appendix for Instrumental Range Chart.) Ensemble music with satisfying results is thus possible from the beginning of music study. Children are drawn to the instruments because they like to play with sound and to master the challenges presented by instrumental parts of various levels of difficulty.

The instrumental ensemble consists of the metal soprano and alto glockenspiels and soprano, alto, and bass metallophones. Soprano, alto, and bass xylophones are made of wood or a wood substitute. The instruments may perform in families or contrasting colors may play together.

Extreme care should be taken when orchestrating instrumental accompaniment for voices. The texture ought to be spare to avoid covering the delicate sound of the children's voices. The texture may., however, be thicker when instruments are played without voices.

Kentucky Mountain Song

V

SG
AG
Recorder

AX

BX

BM

Chick-en crow-in' on Sour-wood Moun-tain, Hey de ding dang dil-ly dal-ly day.

Vol. III, p. 12

Instrumental Piece

SG

SG

AG

AX

Triangle

Timp.

Bass

pizz.

arco

Vol. III, p. 15

Very significant dimensions are added to music learning by the bar instruments. Children see, as well as hear, pitch relationships. They learn by observation a very important principle of sound: larger instruments produce lower sounds. They also learn absolute pitch names from the letters on the bars. And children learn that their individual contribution counts; each part is crucial to the musical whole.

(iv) Recorders and Other Instruments

Orff selected the recorder to provide the melodic voice for many instrumental pieces because the tone quality is well matched with that of the bar instruments. Orff teachers use the recorder for improvising, for playing melodies with the instrumental ensemble, and for performing standard historical repertoire. Many offer the recorder as a part of their music curriculum to reinforce notation skills, to develop musicianship, to teach ensemble performance, and to encourage improvisation. Teachers proficient on krummhorn, shawm, and other early wind instruments also introduce them to their students.

Traditional orchestral instruments may be added to the Orff ensemble if care is taken to balance the voices. The piano may be used sparingly if it is in tune with the instruments and if the outer registers are played. Covering the pitches of the bar instruments should generally be avoided.

The sound of such stringed instruments as guitar, bowed psaltry, bordun cello, and dulcimer are very complementary to the bar instruments. Young children will use them to perform borduns and older students will want to play melodies and chord changes on these instruments.

As we have seen, the range of color possibilities available for the children's use is very wide in an Orff classroom. Although one can actually teach music in this way without the benefit of instruments, the addition of timbre to the music class enhances the other elements. Fine quality instruments perform an invaluable role in the development of children's musical understanding.

Listening

Listening is a skill fostered throughout the child's participation in an Orff program but it is often directed toward activities in which he or she is actively participating. Orff teachers also believe that it is of crucial importance that children hear music which they cannot yet make themselves. The leap from music-making to music-listening is made more relevant to the children if connections between the two can be made.[3]

Meter, form, texture, and such expressive elements as dynamics, color, and tempo provide obvious points of contact between student- and adult-made music. Children who are given a short specific listening task that relates to their own experience become very willing listeners. They welcome aural challenges which are drawn from a wide variety of styles and types of music. In these ways listening takes its place as an indispensable means of developing and extending the conceptual framework and aesthetic awareness of children.

3 · Orff Pedagogy

The aim of fine music-teaching is student mastery of skills and concepts. Orff teachers believe that these are best taught inductively by means of a four-stage learning process: imitation, exploration, literacy and improvisation. This means that all students are given many opportunities to experiment with a wide range of musical problems. From these encounters students can develop the skills and concepts that promote independent musicianship. The order of presentation of the stages illustrates the increasingly complex musical responses required of the students. In the classroom, however, the stages are not hierarchical for overlap will occur at every step and within any lesson. Every link in this learning chain may be connected to every other link so long as it aids in fostering mastery of skills and concepts.

Imitation

(i) Simultaneous Imitation

Some of the processes we use to build skills and concepts in the introductory stages are very similar to those used in traditional teaching methods. Imitation activities, for instance, are a favorite means of helping students of all ages and abilities to develop and build aural skills. Simultaneous imitation is one such device. It occurs when the imitated response happens at virtually the same time as the cue. A typical example is the kind of spontaneous follow-the-leader opportunity found in the 'Simon says' game. This same spontaneous imitation idea is used in movement activities, in body-percussion, sound imitation and in instrumental responses to body-percussion gestures. Here are some examples.

Movement activities provide a typical introduction to simultaneous imitation. While imitating your movements the child builds observation skills, develops the ability to react to cues quickly, and begins to build a movement vocabulary through gross motor activity. Rhythmic pattern and group pulse may also be introduced through simultaneous imitation. Mirror movement, which involves following the gestures of a leader or a partner as they occur, is another typical imitation activity. Because none of these involve sound stimuli, they are especially effective introductions to simultaneous imitation experiences.

Body-percussion sound imitation introduces children to the tone-color possibilities of their own bodies. They can imitate your gestures by clapping, snapping, thigh-patting, and stepping sounds, adding vocal colors if they seem appropriate. Because these sounds provide a variety of colors, they can be orchestrated into little pieces. Thus the groundwork for later layering of vocal and instrumental parts is established.

Instrumental responses to body-percussion gestures involve transferring your movements to pitched or unpitched percussion instruments. For example, a snap of your fingers might be the cue for glockenspiel players to respond. Typical transfers include snaps to the metal unpitched instruments and glockenspiels, claps to wooden unpitched instruments and xylophones, pats to small drums and metallophones, and steps to large drums and bass instruments. This kind of spontaneous sound imitation is particularly well suited to creating sound stories and to providing orchestrations for movement activities.

(ii) Remembered Imitation

Asking children to remember a cue for later performance is a procedure used by most music teachers. This indispensable learning device is called remembered or echo imitation. In echo work the children repeat a gesture, a sound, a rhythm pattern, or a melodic motive exactly as given by the teacher. This is a crucial activity for building tonal and rhythmic memory at every stage of the child's musical development. The response to the initial pattern will be in the same medium as the cue during the early grades. Older children, however, can echo your body-percussion patterns on unpitched percussion instruments; melodies you have sung might be imitated on bar instruments or recorder.

Remembered imitation activities assume special importance as preliminary steps to improvisation and as introductory and evaluation steps in an activity. As we all know, echo work is a convenient way of introducing material which will be used throughout a lesson. But it is also an important means of evaluating student progress. Can the students repeat melodic motives accurately? Can they recognize and perform rhythm phrases which consist of patterns from their current music study? Finally, and most important, can the students lead echo activities?

(iii) Overlapping Imitation

An introduction to overlapping imitation for young children is provided by the 'change at the magic word' game. To begin this activity, you may establish a movement gesture which is imitated by your class. Then continue the game by introducing a new gesture which the class imitates only after you've said the magic word. Children love to assume your leadership role after they are familiar with the game.

Overlapping imitation for older children is easily illustrated in the body-percussion canon. In this activity, the second voice generally follows the first at the interval of four beats. For example, you might begin by clapping ♩ ♫ ♫ ♩ which the students imitate while you continue with a new gesture (thigh-pats) and rhythm. Simple patterns are alternated with more complex ones to help the students succeed. Finger-snapping and stepping may be added as the students are ready for greater challenges. The following score illustrates a typical body percussion canon.

Melodic overlapping imitation is also possible. To clarify statement and response, your motives may be given in a different sound medium from that of the respondents. For instance, you might first play a motive on the recorder, asking the group to repeat it vocally four beats later while you continue to introduce new material. A pentatonic framework is useful at the beginning of this work, though it may be expanded to diatonic as the competence of the students grows. The following score illustrates the melodic imitation idea.

We find that movement is a very useful medium when we wish to provide a graphic illustration of polyphonic texture. Movement canons may be performed without accompaniment, or groups may be assigned a sound-color cue. In either case, half of the class should perform for the other half so that the idea of overlapping imitation is made clear through visual reinforcement.

Let us summarize: three types of imitation activities which we have considered – simultaneous, remembered, and overlapping – provide essential introductions to the elements of music and to the various media which the children use in their music-making. And, most important, the children become familiar with the Orff style of participatory activity which is so fundamental to their further musical development.

Exploration

The Orff teacher is always seeking opportunities to challenge the students to find new ways to use the musical materials they are learning. These experiments in musical exploration are important steps toward improvisation. Encourage your students to participate in the composition process by experimenting with changes in such expressive elements as dynamics, accent, color, and tempo. 'Can you play that pattern twice as fast?' 'How would our melody sound if we sang it softer?' 'How do you think the melody would sound if we played it on a xylophone instead of the recorder?' are the sorts of questions which encourage this kind of exploration.

But expressive elements are not the only resource for experimentation. Other elements of music may provide useful variation devices for your students. For example, they may want to try increasing or decreasing rhythmic activity in a musical phrase, or changing the meter of a composition. Perhaps altering the direction of a melody, or increasing or decreasing the melodic activity, or changing registers will interest them. Or they might want to experiment by moving the tonal center from *do* to *la* to see how the piece sounds in minor. They can try to enrich the texture of their piece by adding instruments on each repetition of the melody. The possibilities for development are limited only by the imagination, skill, and resources of you and your class. Orff classrooms are alive with this sense of discovery because students are constantly being challenged to manipulate musical ideas in original ways. Because concepts are formed as students use musical elements in their own work, this stage in the learning process is of critical importance.

Literacy

Orff teachers have no rigidly prescribed system of teaching musical literacy. In fact, Carl Orff viewed the early emphasis on literacy as a cause of, not a solution for, unmusical music pedagogy. He pointed out that children were being taught symbols of notation before they had learned to speak in music, much as if they had no language facility before they were taught to read. Orff's alternative approach offered the ideas and instrumental apparatus to learn to speak in music; introduction to notation then became a necessary later learning step. As Orff observed at the Toronto symposium in 1962, 'It is not difficult to convince a child of the need for notation, particularly if continuous improvisation creates the desire to keep a record of the melodies invented. In the long run it is not possible to make progress without knowing notation.'[1]

American Orff teachers have taken an approach to literacy in which experience with sound always precedes the introduction of its iconic representation. Sound before symbol is the general rule. The idea that symbols can represent sounds is established with young children through the use of graphic notation. Graphic scores lead naturally to the introduction of contemporary notation devices in the upper grades. These scores are generally realized using vocal sounds and pitched or unpitched percussion instruments.

Here is an example of a graphic score intended for performance by primary children.

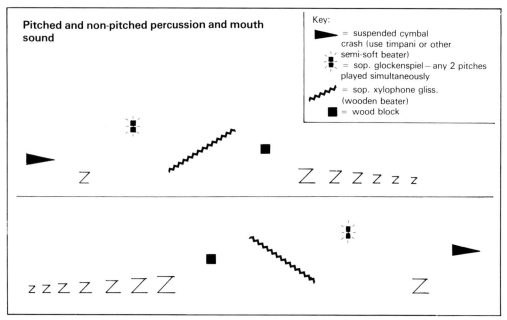

Vol. I, p. 51

Conventional notation is introduced through rhythm symbols in most Orff classrooms. Children are initially taught the symbols for the quarter note, its equivalent rest, and its division. The symbols are presented in the context of an established pulse which is played on the body and unpitched instruments, stepped in place, and stepped in space. Thus the relationship of rhythmic pattern to pulse is established at the outset.

Pitch notation is introduced using a limited number of tones. The falling minor third (*sol-mi*) and the three-note *mi-re-do* are typical points of departure; pitches are added in succession according to the preference of the teacher. One possible sequence of presentation of pitches is given in Part Two of this book. Assimilation of the entire pentatonic scale is usually assumed at the end of Second Grade, competence in reading and writing the full diatonic scale by the end of Fourth Grade.

The tonal and visual reinforcement of pitch symbols provided by the bar instruments is a great help to young music-readers. Learning absolute pitch names in the intermediate grades is greatly facilitated by letter names on bar instruments.

Improvisation

As we have seen in this chapter, imitation, exploration, and notation of musical elements are important preliminary steps to improvisation because students need skills on which to draw for their original work. Because exploration involves *altering* some element of known material and improvisation requires *inventing* new musical ideas, improvisation is usually the culminating activity in the teaching sequence at every stage of music learning. In improvisation, as in no other class activity, the students demonstrate their musical independence from the teacher.

Students may be asked to improvise using a variety of musical elements and Orff media depending upon the level of skill which they have acquired. For example, such an unstructured activity as movement improvisation to sound cues may occur at all levels, but the response of a first-grader is likely to be much different from that of a fourth-grade student. Visual and dramatic imagery also provide stimuli for movement response and for instrumental improvisation. Or, to turn the response into a stimulus, movement itself can generate vocal and instrumental melodic or sound color improvisations.

Form is the element which provides the Orff teacher with an abundance of improvisation opportunities. From phrase building using question-answer technique to improvising entire contrasting sections, it is this experience of creating something new within a given structure that offers students the challenge, and the satisfaction, of making original contributions to the ensemble.

The child's first attempts at creating form usually consist of making up melodic or rhythmic motives. These patterns can be developed into a phrase, or a series of phrases, and finally into a little form. Rhythmic and melodic question and answer is another phrase-building activity used by Orff teachers. In this activity you may play ♫ ♩ ♩ ♩ and the child might answer ♫ ♩ ♩ 𝄽. Asking the class to repeat both the question and the answer offers the chance to assimilate the entire phrase and to involve everyone actively in the improvisation process. This same procedure may be used to create phrases using vocal sounds (vocables), sung pitches, bar instruments, and recorder. The phrases will increase in length and complexity as the children's skill grows.

Of course, we want to avoid exercise for its own sake. That is why phrase-building activities are generally conducted within a context; they should lead somewhere. The new phrase may be used as an introduction or coda to a piece the children already know, or it might provide contrasting sections to a given theme in a rondo, or it might be the first phrase in an entirely new composition. Whatever its later use, you will find your students delighted to realize that their contributions are sufficiently valued to be incorporated into a larger work. Older students will be prepared through phrase-building activities to devise larger sections for pieces. Creating a B section for a given A to develop a ternary form is one possible example of this idea.

Evaluation of the children's musical development is easily accomplished in improvisation situations. You will have no trouble noting the various ability levels in the class and determining skills which need remedial work. Children who have played with the elements of music, who have listened with care to the efforts of their classmates, and who have learned to make musical choices have taken important steps toward becoming independent musicians.

4 · Orff Theory

It is the theoretical aspect of Orff-Schulwerk about which there has been the most confusion and misrepresentation in American music education methods, texts, and song series books. Because the only handbook of 'elemental style' available to teachers was published more than twenty years ago, contemporary application of the style has not yet been documented.[1] Workshops, summer courses, and a few published collections of materials have, therefore, been the primary sources of information about the theoretical principles of Orff musical practice. While it is beyond the scope of this book to offer a complete review of Orff theory, it is essential for teachers to become familiar with terms and stylistic principles which are commonly used in Orff classrooms.

The term 'elemental style' describes the unique treatment of musical elements introduced by Carl Orff in the musical examples presented in the original volumes of *Music for Children*.[2] Characteristic features of the style introduced in Volume One include the use of repeated rhythmic or melodic patterns known as ostinati, tonic (pedal) or tonic and fifth (bordun) accompaniment, and anhemitonic (without half-steps) pentatonic melodies. Let us examine each of these devices in greater detail.

Ostinati

Orff knew that children find security in repetition. This is one reason why repeated patterns known as ostinati provide the basic accompaniment framework in Orff-Schulwerk. Orff teachers generally understand ostinato to mean a rhythmic, melodic, or harmonic pattern which is repeated.[3] They find that the ostinato offers the child the opportunity to play and sing in ensemble at an early age. Because there is rhythmic independence and tension between the parts, the children become familiar with fundamental principles of composition from the beginning of their music study. Aural awareness is fostered by discovering the relationship of one part to another in the ensemble. Finally, musical memory, rhythmic independence, and coordination are developed as children are asked to master parts which increasingly challenge their musical abilities. For all of these reasons the ostinato device pervades all media at all levels of instruction.

(i) Movement Ostinati
These patterns may be structured or free and the performers organized in sections or in a solo/chorus arrangement. The verse 'Giants' provides an example of a speech activity which readily lends itself to movement and a movement ostinato accompaniment for young children.[4] One group steps the

rhythm and speaks the text of the verse while the other performs the ostinato. The text 'fee, fi, fo, fum' spoken while stepping half notes is one ostinato possibility. As in all Orff activities, musical learning is enhanced if the groups change roles.

Long steps, strong steps, moving right along steps,

Long steps, strong steps, here the giants come.

Music for Children Vol. I, p. 22

(ii) Speech ostinati

Speech provides the opportunity to develop rhythmic security while layering accompaniment ostinati. Patterns which complement one another as well as the text encourage rhythmic independence and produce a pleasing musical result. The following short example illustrates this point.

Old Mother Witch

arr. JF

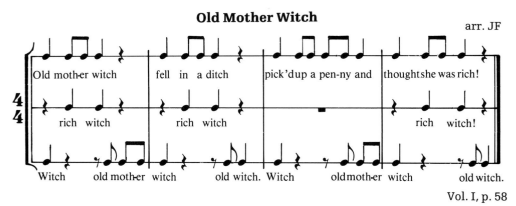

Vol. I, p. 58

Speech activities also include vocal sounds known as vocables. They provide a wealth of possibilities for exploring rhythm and color in group ensembles. An example for intermediate children is:

Tik Booda Tsay Hi

JF

(iii) Sung ostinati

The ostinato provides the easiest entrance to vocal independence for young

34

singers. It is particularly successful in the early stages when both voices begin on a unison pitch and when the vocal ostinato pattern is relatively short. It must have a rhythmic and melodic life of its own, separate from that of the melody. The example which follows can be performed by young singers.

Pretty Little Baby

arr. JF

What you gon-na call your pret-ty lit-tle ba - by? What you gon-na call your pret-ty lit-tle ba - by?

Ba - by, ba - by bye. Ba - by, ba - by bye.

What you gon-na call your pret-ty lit-tle ba - by? Born, born in Beth-le - hem.

Ba - by, ba - by bye. Ba - by, ba - by bye.

Vol. I, p. 46

(iv) Instrumental ostinati

These accompaniments fall into three categories: body percussion, unpitched percussion, and pitched percussion. They may support spoken or sung texts, rhythmic phrases, or instrumental melodies. Because examples are so readily available, only one illustration is offered here.

Chatter with the Angels

arr. JF

Clap

Pat

Step

Vol. II, p.66

It is obvious from the following example how readily transfer can be made from one media to another. The children learn all the constituent layers of a composition when pitched and unpitched parts are first prepared on the body and later performed on instruments. They discover that their interesting musical pieces result from interweaving rhythmic and melodic voices; thus, they are engaged in authentic group music experiences at all levels. It is only a small step from this knowledge to understanding examples of art music beyond their performance abilities.

arr. JF

Chat-ter with the an-gels soon in the morn-ing, chat-ter with the an-gels in that land.

The ostinato is treated in motivic fashion in the original volumes of *Music for Children*. Recent composition in elemental style, however, demonstrates a strong tendency toward construction of ostinato patterns based on phrases and combined in a contrapuntal style. Further changes from the original models include combining patterns of different lengths, emphasizing complementary rhythms among the voices, and creating a rather spare, open texture in the accompaniment. The reader will have no trouble finding examples in this book and others which illustrate this evolution of elemental style.

Melody

The melodic material in Volume One of Orff's *Music for Children* is *do*-centered pentatonic. Using scales without half-steps helps students to make simple accompaniments, sing in tune and improvise. Furthermore, a wealth of traditional American music now becomes accessible to students, hence the cultural heritage is explored as music is taught.

Three *do* pentatonic scales and their *la*-centered relatives are in general use among Orff teachers. Instrument playing and sight-singing are facilitated through the use of C, F, and G and their related a, d, and e scales because no accidentals are involved with these keys.

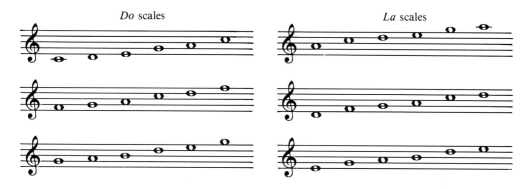

It is also possible to play *do* pentatonics on D and B-flat and related *la* scales on b and g with the use of chromatic bars.

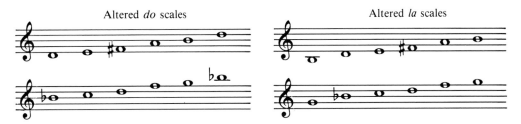

Altered *do* scales   Altered *la* scales

You may also wish to explore pentatonic scales in which *re, mi,* or *sol* serve as the tonal center. Although the folk heritage offers few examples of these rather obscure pentatonics, they provide interesting improvisation challenges for older children.

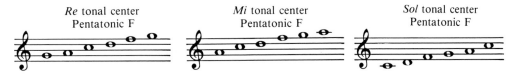

Re tonal center   *Mi* tonal center   *Sol* tonal center
Pentatonic F   Pentatonic F   Pentatonic F

Addition of the fourth and seventh scale degrees, in succession, completes the diatonic scale. Volume Two of *Music for Children* provides examples of these melodies.

Hexatonic   Diatonic

The last two volumes of *Music for Children* include examples of aeolian, phrygian, and dorian modes. Mixolydian and lydian modes are considered in a later volume entitled *Paralipomena*.[5]

It is evident from the sequence of the volumes that Orff presented his modal material in major/minor categories. Following this approach and working from a pentatonic cell greatly facilitates the teaching of modes. The cell itself is constant in all *do* modes and in all *la* modes; the remaining scale tones provide the particular intervals characteristic of each.[6]

Major Modes

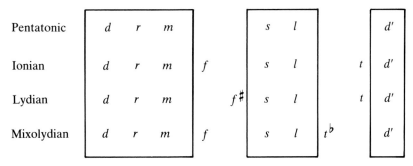

Pentatonic	*d*	*r*	*m*			*s*	*l*		*d'*
Ionian	*d*	*r*	*m*	*f*		*s*	*l*	*t*	*d'*
Lydian	*d*	*r*	*m*		*f*♯	*s*	*l*	*t*	*d'*
Mixolydian	*d*	*r*	*m*	*f*		*s*	*l*	*t*♭	*d'*

Minor Modes

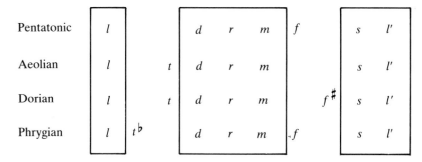

Pentatonic	*l*			*d*	*r*	*m*	*f*	*s* *l'*
Aeolian	*l*		*t*	*d*	*r*	*m*		*s* *l'*
Dorian	*l*		*t*	*d*	*r*	*m*	*f*#	*s* *l'*
Phrygian	*l*	*t*♭		*d*	*r*	*m*	*f*	*s* *l'*

Pedals and Borduns

Pedal tones on the tonic are the simplest means of providing tonal stability in elemental style accompaniments. This accompaniment device is introduced in the earliest stages of Orff work.

Three Wise Men of Gotham

arr. JF

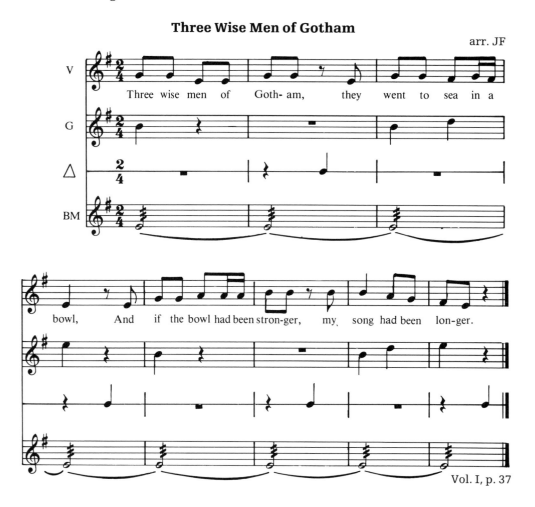

Three wise men of Goth- am, they went to sea in a bowl, And if the bowl had been stron-ger, my song had been lon-ger.

Vol. I, p. 37

38

The simple bordun is the foundation of the elemental accompaniment style. It is fashioned from the first and fifth scale degrees in the same octave and it is played below the melody on strong beats. The resulting sound, somewhat like the drone of a bagpipe, supports the tonal center in a non-functional harmonic manner.

Page's Train

Orff provided models of three variations of this two-note chord bordun. The first, called a level bordun, involves a change in registers.

Page's Train

Another alternative is to play the first and fifth scale tones in succession. This is termed a broken bordun.

Page's Train

American/ arr. JF

Finally, the broken bordun may be arpeggiated.

Page's Train

American/ arr. JF

Examples of some of the many possible rhythmic variations of these bordun styles may be found in Part Two of this book.

Moving Bordun

The first tentative step away from the strong foundation provided by the simple bordun is movement of one of the two tones to an adjacent pitch. For example, the fifth moves *up* to the sixth or *down* to the fourth scale degree returning to the bordun on strong beats.[7] The second example illustrates decoration of the fifth in both directions.[8]

Sieben kleine Spielstücke

Pentatonic treatment of the moving fifth is slightly different from that of the diatonic. The fourth scale degree is avoided in the accompaniment because it is not present in the melody. Thus the lower neighbor used for decoration in pentatonic is the third scale degree. The bass xylophone part illustrates the embellished fifth in *la*-centered pentatonic in the following example.

Listen to the Lambs

American/ arr. JF

Lis-ten to the lambs All a cry-ing! Lis-ten to the lambs All a-cry-ing!

Lis-ten to the lambs All a-cry-ing! Want to go to hea-ven when I die!

A complete definition of moving bordun includes movement of the first, as well as the fifth, scale degree. In this case, the movement is handled with considerable care to avoid weakening the tonal stability. Isolated examples of double moving borduns supporting diatonic melodies may also be found. However, the pre eminence of the tonic tonal center is threatened by moving the first and fifth scale degrees together, hence, the use of the double moving bordun is very rare.

Other Accompaniments

Volumes Two to Five of *Music for Children* provide a wealth of examples of shifting triad and functional harmonic accompaniment in elemental style. A review of the contents of the five volumes reveals that Orff proceeded very carefully from drone (bordun) in Volume One to shifting triad and functional accompaniment styles in subsequent volumes.

Volume	Melody	Accompaniment
I	*do* pentatonic	bordun
II	hexatonic, diatonic major	moving bordun I-ii I-vi
III	diatonic major	I-V I-IV-V
IV	aeolian, phrygian, dorian modes	bordun i-VII i-III
V	aeolian, harmonic minor	dominant triad (minor third) dominant triad (major third) subdominant in minor
Paralipomena	lydian, mixolydian modes	accompaniments from Vols I-IV

American teachers have found that elemental accompaniment styles are well suited to the wide variety of folk literature available in their culture. Recent settings of this material demonstrate a highly selective use of instrumental color to enhance, rather than cover, the children's singing voices. The following examples of settings of American material are offered to illustrate this point.

The I-ii progression is the first step away from bordun accompaniment. It is created by adding the third to the double moving bordun and it shares the non-functional coloristic qualities and close association to the tonic with the moving bordun. In fact, the tonic is typically retained in the bass in a I-ii setting, while the alto voice provides the triad movement from tonic (on strong beats) to supertonic on weak beats. Because of this triadic texture in the singing range, use of the I-ii with voices is somewhat limited. Here is an example of this progression in an American folk song accompaniment.

Mama Don't 'Low

Trad./ arr. JF

Ma-ma don't 'low no pick-in' and sing-in' round here.

Ma-ma don't 'low no pick-in' and sing-in' round here.

We don't care what Ma-ma don't 'low, Gon-na pick and sing a-ny how.

Ma-ma don't 'low no pick-in' and sing-in' round here.

This is an example of a I-vi shifting triad accompaniment in elemental style.

Hush Little Baby (I)

American/arr. JF

Hush lit-tle ba - by, don't you cry, Dad-dy will come home bye and bye.

This example illustrates functional I-V treatment of a pentatonic melody. It is followed by a I-IV-V blues progression orchestrated for Orff instruments.

Lelia

American/arr. JF

Le - lia, that's shoe my love, Le - lia, that's shoe my love.

Turn me in a hur - ry now, shoe ba - by, shoe my love.

Good Morning Blues

H. Ledbetter/arr. JF

1. Good morn-in' blues, Blues how do you do? Good
2. Called yes-ter day, Here you come to – Called

Doo doodoodoodoodoodoo

morn – in' blues, Blues how do you do? I'm
yes – ter day. Here you come to – day. Your

doo. Doo doodoodoo doodoodoo

do-in' all right, Good morn-in' how are you?
mouth's wide o-pen but you don't know what to say.

doo Doo doo doodoo doodoo

i-VII and i-III are shifting triads used to accompany minor melodies. Here is
an example of each.

To the Pines

American/arr. JF

Look down, look down that lone — some road, Hang
pines, to the pines, where the sun ne — ver shines, And I

down your head and cry. To the
shiv-er when cold winds blow.

Hush Little Baby (II)

American/arr. JF

1. Hush lit-tle ba — by, don't say a word, Pa-pa's gon-na buy you a mock-ing bird.
2. It can whistle and it can sing. It can do most an — y-thing.

The last example shows functional treatment of a harmonic minor melody.

The Lonely Dove

American/arr. JF

I hear the voice of the lone-ly dove Coo coo coo, his notes are so clear. He

sings a song to his la – dy love, To tell her he'll al-ways be near._____

With the completion of this survey of Orff-Schulwerk practice we can now proceed to our central task: the design of a curriculum that will not only engage our students but will help them master the skills and concepts necessary for developing independent musicianship.

Part Two:

ORFF-SCHULWERK IN PRACTICE

All music teachers who face the practicalities of limited space, equipment, budget, and time know they must order their priorities. What is to be taught, in what order, and by what means? We Orff teachers, of course, share this responsibility with our professional colleagues, but we find the issue considerably more complicated by the wide variety of means available to us. For instance, certain note values must be taught. Is this best accomplished through movement, a speech activity, a song or a pitched or unpitched percussion composition? How do we order these activities for presentation to the children? What means should be used to determine whether the children have mastered a particular skill or concept?

These questions have not been fully answered by Orff teachers because most of us have found developing and teaching musical activities to be a more congenial task than organizing the vast amount of material into a developmental framework. Also, we have been cautious about following organizational schemes which might turn the freshness of Orff's ideas into yet another rigid method for teaching music.

My own experience, however, suggests that the effect of using a curriculum outline is not at all restrictive. It encourages me to use the abundance of Orff media available to reach the various levels of interest and talent of the children I teach, as well as the goals of my program.

The sequence presented in this book has evolved from many years of classroom experience as an Orff teacher. The order of presentation changes somewhat each year, and the supporting activities for each step of the sequence are *always* changed to accommodate the strengths and weaknesses of different groups of students.

However, some words of advice are in order. First, only a few of the many possible activities that might be used to support each step are offered in this book; each of you should supplement my material with your own favorites. In addition, your particular area of musical expertise can add much to the experience of your children. Chorus, recorder, folk-dance, and drama are among the possible additions to this curriculum.

Second, the presentation of each step is only the beginning of mastery. We need to return again and again to earlier steps to assure that what has been taught can be applied in new situations. The ability to transfer skills and understandings is, of course, the ultimate test of musical independence.

Third, the sequence for each grade presents only music which children can learn to read and write. You should therefore introduce additional rhythmic material and rote songs that provide challenges beyond the notation skills of your students. Obviously, this music can be great fun and it has the added merit of preparing your class for future learning.

And last is the matter of time and numbers. In my school, each music class receives seventy to eighty minutes of instruction per week. Given that amount of time and no more than fifteen to twenty students it is possible to accomplish the sequence for each grade. Yet what if your time is much less or your class size much larger? Or both? Then simply move through the steps at a slower pace. Should you be fortunate enough to have more time and smaller classes you might consider a faster tempo. But in all cases we need to remember that there is no exact way of calculating music instruction. Nothing is easier – and more destructive – than to overwhelm students with challenges they can't meet. But it is also destructive to settle for too little. The task for us is to find the proper mix; it is not an easy one.

5 · Grade One: Beginning at the Beginning

With this chapter we start the process of translating Orff's intentions into an actual program of instruction. Media, pedagogy and theory are now combined in a step-by-step process designed to show students how to use their inherent musicality to become independent musicians. In Grade One we begin by setting ourselves eight major goals.

1. Our first aim, and one that remains an objective throughout the elementary years, is to teach children the conventions of group participation.

2. To introduce a rudimentary music vocabulary. This early, and continuous, emphasis on vocabulary is important as young students desire and need to know the terminology of the art they are studying.

3. To introduce children to such indispensable musical elements as rhythm and tone color. We begin by developing beat competency, indispensable to the study of rhythm; soon the class should be able to combine beat and rhythm to make simple compositions.

4. To help children develop rhythmic and tonal memory. The first two steps take up the former, the last two take up the latter.

5. To learn rhythmic notation. This new challenge has been delayed until now so as to be certain that your students have had enough experience with rhythm and beat to understand the need to remember them through notation.

6. To teach some of the intricacies of accompaniment, after your students are comfortable with the notation of simple rhythms.

7. To focus on melody, specifically pitch syllables. As we all know, singing in tune is difficult for many young children. Consequently, only after most of the class has met this challenge do we introduce pitch syllables. As usual in Orff instruction, instruments as well as singing are employed to reinforce mastery and retention. By this time the majority of your students should be able to sing, play and improvise with five pitches.

8. We complete the year's work with a listening exercise. Our principal aim is to show students the connection between their own skills and understandings on the one hand and the vast world of more complex music on the other. Showing this relationship is particularly important because even young students can be brought to see that they are actually part of a much larger musical culture. In the process your class also gets a chance to review such first year fundamentals as listening and remembering, group work and rhythmic notation. Finally, this exercise foreshadows the further work on sectional form that continues in Grades Two and Three. Hence this last step provides a convenient bridge to the year ahead.

Listed below are the goals for the year and the steps designed to accomplish them.

Group Participation

1 Perform simultaneous imitation using movement, instruments, and vocal sounds

Vocabulary

1 Distinguish faster from slower tempi
2 Distinguish louder from softer dynamics
3 Use bar and unpitched instruments as sound-carpets for stories
4 Identify phrases in spoken texts and in simple songs

Rhythm and Tone Color

1 Perform beath (speak, pat, clap, play, and step)
2 Explore speech material for inflection, improvisation, and rhythm
3 Transfer text rhythm to sound color (body percussion and unpitched percussion) to distinguish rhythm from beat
4 Create rhythmic compositions using texts

Rhythm and Tonal Memory

1 Imitate movement motives in place; later in space
2 Imitate rhythmic motives (body percussion and unpitched instruments)
3 Distinguish higher from lower pitches. Sing and locate pitches on instruments
4 Echo-sing melodic motives

Rhythm Notation

1 Read, clap, and play ♩ ♫ ♩
2 Identify ❙ , ❙ and ostinato
3 Create one, then two voice rhythm pieces using ♩ ♫ ♩

Accompaniment

1 Perform the beat simultaneously with a spoken text
2 Sing melody and play the beat simultaneously
3 Add a simple tonic accompaniment to appropriate melodies
4 Accompany appropriate song material with simple bordun played on bar instruments as a chord on strong beats
5 Accompany appropriate song material with level bordun
6 Add a second complementary sound color to bordun accompaniment for songs
7 Accompany song material with broken bordun accompaniment. A second complementary sound color and/or an unpitched percussion part may be added

Melody

1 Imitate, then improvise melodies vocally and on instruments using the *mi re do* motive. Add a simple tonic accompaniment
2 Play aural recognition games using the *mi re do* syllables

3 Add tone syllable names to rhythm syllables as a step toward music reading

4 Introduce *sol* and *la* pitches to complete the pentatonic scale vocabulary. Identify specific intervals from this scale isolated from song literature; add tonic and bordun accompaniments

Listening

1 Sing, play, and listen to music in binary (AB) form

Group Participation

1 Perform simultaneous imitation using movement, instruments and vocal sounds

I have found that simultaneous imitation is the best way to begin the musical education of small children. By copying the teacher, students quickly learn a vocabulary of instrumental, vocal, body, and percussion sounds. With this vocabulary they are now able to invent the musical equivalent of sentences and paragraphs. Within days average students are aware that they possess this creative ability and nothing is more self-affirming or contributes more to a growing desire to learn. Secondly, much of the joy of musical creation comes from cooperating with others; simultaneous imitation introduces students from the very first day of class to the importance of this shared effort. Thirdly, there is no activity better designed to give a sense of immediacy and to hold attention than the effort to reproduce quickly and accurately the sounds of the leader. Lastly, when *students* lead the class they become responsible for inventing sound and movement ideas of their own. They are thereby taking the first small steps towards the competent musicianship which is the ultimate goal of all our efforts in music education. An easy introduction to this activity is the well-known 'Simon says' game. You may soon eliminate the direction 'Simon says do this' and invite the children to follow your cues without a verbal invitation.

Movement. It is a good idea to do only in-place movement activities at first because you then reduce the complexities with which your class must deal when responding to an external stimulus. An excellent way to begin is to invite the class to imitate your facial expressions and your body movements as you contrast high and low, round and angular, wide and narrow, and the like. Exploration of body parts is accomplished in place. Hands, shoulders, head, knees, and a variety of other parts can be used to express such things as the movements of animals, marionettes, and machines. Your students will also enjoy illustrating simple rhymes and poems with their bodies. For instance, one child may serve as the clock for her partner's mouse in *Hickory Dickory Dock*. In this case, of course, the movement cues are verbal.

Locomotor movements take the child from place to space. Walking, running, skipping, hopping, galloping, and jumping should be unpatterned at first, but later can be used to illustrate changes in tempo, accent, and dynamics, or to show phrase length. Sound signals may be employed to initiate or terminate locomotor movements. Quick response to these cues builds aural attention which is a prerequisite for musical development.

A more challenging level of response is required when you give one sound signal – made by a drum, for instance – to suggest a given locomotor movement and another – a cymbal, say – for a contrasting in-place activity. This kind of exercise not only heightens aural acuity but is also great fun.

Instruments. The use of the body as an instrument offers children the opportunity to experience timbre at a very basic level. Either you or your students may lead non-patterned clapping, thigh-patting, or stepping. Next, demonstrate the color contrasts of tuned and untuned percussion instruments through simultaneous responses by the children to your instrumental cues.

Pitched or unpitched percussion instruments may also be assigned a corresponding body sound with the children responding on instruments which match your body instrument cues. For example, you might snap your fingers for glockenspiels or triangles, clap for xylophones or woodblocks, pat thighs for metallophones or hand drums, and step for bass instruments or tympani. Because the cue here is in a different medium from the response, two colors are sufficient at first. Spontaneous instrumental pieces created in this way are especially effective when used as sound settings for poetry and stories. Students particularly enjoy this activity when they have the opportunity to lead the instrumental players.

Vocal Sounds. Vocal sound experiments give children the opportunity to investigate the many color possibilities in the human voice. Various effects with the tongue and lips such as clicking and hissing are among the many colors which can be spontaneously created. These, together with sirens and vowel sounds at various pitch levels (which are excellent preparation for singing) may be used to portray natural sounds such as water and wind, or machinery such as elevators and roller-coasters.

Vocal sounds may be used as background color for a rhyme, poem or song, or they may be organized into a little piece. An example enjoyed by my children is *Humpty Dumpty*.

> Humpty Dumpty sat on a wall (sigh – in a relaxed way)
> Humpty Dumpty had a great fall (voice falls – 'ahhhhh')
> All the king's horses (tongue clicks in galloping rhythm)
> And all the king's men (clear throats with authority)
> Couldn't put Humpty together again (sad 'ooooooo')

Eventually, in the final performance, the vocal sounds are performed without the text.

Vocabulary

1 Distinguish faster from slower tempi

One of our goals in this first year of instruction is the introduction of an elementary music vocabulary. Young children should therefore become familiar with the expressive elements of music at the beginning of their music study. They can then apply the concepts of tempo and dynamics to their subsequent music experience.

Tempo may be introduced by using all of the typical Orff media discussed in Chapter Two. You might begin by asking a student to walk around the room at a regular pace. Then have a second child walk at a new tempo, and call on the class to decide which student is moving faster or slower. Next, ask a child with a pair of claves to create a code signal. Have another child answer this signal with a drum in a new tempo. Again, the children determine whether the second was faster or slower than the first.

Another rhyme which lends itself to exploration of tempo contrast is *Linnery, Lannery, Lock*.[1]

> Linnery, lannery, lock
> The shoe walks along with the sock
> The pants and the shirt ran away with the skirt
> Linnery, lannery, lock

Encourage one student to say the second line at a different tempo from the group's initial 'Linnery, lannery, lock'. A second child then provides a contrasting tempo to that of the first. There are, of course, many variations you might explore.

Other poems, rhymes and songs will provide your students with endless opportunities to become familiar with this concept.

2 Distinguish louder from softer dynamics

In this step, as in the preceding one, your children are adding to their musical vocabulary and conceptual knowledge. Here we focus on the louder-softer contrast in order to distinguish it from – and avoid confusion with – higher-lower to be discussed below.

Begin by having your children experiment by playing a variety of unpitched percussion instruments at different dynamic levels. For instance, they might create a short line of various instruments playing from softest to loudest. The concept can further be reinforced by demonstrating soundless 'loud' and 'soft' movements with the body to show the contrast in intensity. Another effective and enjoyable technique is to play the humming game, a simple variation of 'hot and cold'. Here's how it's played: send one child from the room while an object is hidden. When the child returns, have the rest of the class help by raising or lowering the dynamic level of its humming as the student gets closer to, or farther from, the mystery object. This game also provides you with an excellent opportunity to introduce the term crescendo. Adding voices, either singly or in groups, to a familiar song or poem is another interesting way for children to experience crescendo. Decrescendo results when voices are subtracted from the ensemble. Another effective way to distinguish between loud and soft is to contrast one voice against the group. Individuals, as well as the group, should perform poems, songs and rhymes at various dynamic levels. The need for such materials provides you with an excellent opportunity to ask your students to contribute songs and poems from their own ethnic backgrounds. With any luck at all, this can be a particularly enriching experience for everyone.

3 Use bar and unpitched instruments as sound-carpets for stories

This step, like those before it, lays the foundation for the later musical development of your class. Specifically, students now begin learning to play the instruments they will use throughout their elementary music education.

As your students become familiar with the sound potential of the various instruments used singly and in combination, they will enjoy selecting colors appropriate to the dramatic potential of a story. Aesop's fable *The Wind and the Sun* provides a good opportunity for such experimentation. Aesop has the wind and the sun each claiming to be the stronger. Finally, the sun suggests that they settle the matter in a practical way.

'Do you see that traveller approaching down the road?' asks the sun. 'Let us agree that whichever of us can make the traveller remove his coat will be declared the stronger.'

The wind agrees to these terms and begins to blow as hard as he can. But the harder he blows, the more tightly the traveller wraps his coat about him. Finally, the wind gives up in disgust. The sun then proceeds to shine in all his glory upon the traveller, who finally slumps beneath the shade of a tree and removes his coat. For Aesop, this meant that kindness is more effective than force. However, if your children are like mine, they will love trying to guess the answer and making suggestions of their own. They will also enjoy finding appropriate sounds to accompany this tale. Sometimes the sounds provide a background for the storyteller and sometimes the sounds themselves tell the story. And again, as in step 3, your students may very well have story suggestions of their own to make. These contributions, along with their musical offerings, obviously help children to feel good about themselves and about music.

4 Identify phrases in spoken texts and in simple songs

Identification of the phrase as a complete musical idea cannot begin too early. Conceptualization of the entity of the phrase is a prerequisite to understanding musical form. Introductory activities which offer some concrete possibilities for exploring this concept are outlined below.

Speech. Review the nursery rhyme *Baa Baa Blacksheep*. Divide the group into two sections. Each section speaks its phrase as follows.

> Section 1 Baa baa blacksheep, have you any wool?
> Yes, sir, yes, sir, three bags full.
> Section 2 One for my master, one for my dame.
> One for the little boy who lives in the lane.
> Repeat Section 1.

Movement. In two circles, hands joined, each section steps its eight-beat phrase while saying the text. The first circle repeats its movement to illustrate the form of the text. Introduce the theme from Twelve Variations of *Ah, vous dirais-je, Maman,* K. 265 by Mozart.

The sections may now step to the music, reflecting the identical phrase lengths of the rhyme and the musical example.

Song/Instruments. Children may sing *Twinkle, Twinkle, Little Star* in sections to reinforce the idea of phrase length. The melodic rhythm may be transferred to two different groups of unpitched percussion instruments, each performing its phrase in turn.

Rhythm and Tone Color

1 Perform beat (speak, pat, clap, play, and step)

Our second major objective in this first year of instruction is to introduce students to such fundamental elements of music as rhythm and tone color. Developing beat competency – our purpose in this step – is, of course, preliminary to the study of rhythm and is also a prerequisite for ensemble music-making, another major goal of this grade. Many Orff teachers may have the opportunity to develop this competency with their kindergarten children, but if independence has not been established by the first grade, it needs to be practiced using a variety of media. For example, jump-rope rhymes and jingles provide a rich source of material for developing beat security. Here is an example appropriate for this initial experience because it contains only one sound per beat.

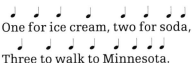

After the rhyme is learned, ask the children to pat their thighs while speaking. The next step involves patting thighs without speaking the text. Your class should speak and clap, and clap without speaking before they attempt to step the rhyme. They may wish to play the rhyme on unpitched percussion instruments and divide the tasks of playing and stepping among two groups. Each of these activities helps to reinforce accuracy of beat response.

2 Explore speech material for inflection, improvisation, and rhythm

In this step we take advantage of the virtual universality of speech to encourage a variety of musical responses from the class. Specifically, speech is used to enhance rhythmic competence and tone color awareness. The following examples illustrate some of the ways texts and words can be used to develop such skills.

Inflection. In and out, round about
O-u-t and that spells out.[2]

This text offers the children a delightful opportunity to experiment with changing the pitch and tone color of the speaking voice. The dynamic level should be kept constant while each word or group of words is changed. Try high, medium, and low ranges, nasal production, and the like. A good introduction to this activity is to select secretly individual children to say the movement words (in, out, round about) using their natural voices. The remaining children listen with their eyes closed and guess the identity of the mystery speakers.

Improvisation. Rain talk: Pitter Patter Chatter.[3] The children may use the expressive elements which they have learned (fast/slow, loud/soft) to say the words in a number of different ways. They may then choose to build a crescendo of word sounds, to add new words to create a rainstorm, or to experiment with creating a word composition. One example among the infinite number of possible results is:

Pitter patter chitter chatter, Pit pat chitter chat.

Rhythm. Shimmy Shimmy Shimmy Pop. Invite your students to say 'pop' in a variety of expressive ways in steady quarter notes. Contrast the one sound of pop (♩) with the two sounds of shimmy (♫) without introducing the symbols. While you keep the beat, have the children choose one word or the other to say in turn around the circle. Now one student may be chosen to conduct a group of four who say the two words in a sequence which they develop themselves.

3 Transfer text rhythm to sound color (body percussion and unpitched percussion) to distinguish rhythm from beat

Combining two distinct colors helps children visualize, hear, perform, and distinguish beat from rhythm. I use this verse as a starting point.[4]

Jelly in the bowl,
Jelly in the bowl,
Wiggle waggle wiggle waggle
Jelly in the bowl.

Have the children first say the text, adding movement wiggle waggles at the appropriate time. Then say the first two and the last lines but substitute movement for the third. These activities establish the length of the phrases and illustrate the form.

At this point the text rhyme can be clapped or patted on thighs. Next ask the children to think the words and to play the beat on the floor or on desks. The challenge is, of course, to end simultaneously on the sixteenth beat. The group divided now performs the beat and the word rhythms simultaneously.

Transfer from body percussion to unpitched instruments is relatively easy to accomplish. Students may select two contrasting groups of instruments (claves and hand drums, for example) on which to perform the beat and the word rhythms. A further step which is very satisfying for children is to add a third sound to the rhythm pattern on the quarter note as follows:

Jelly in the bowl

	Claves	Triangle
Word rhythm:	♫ ♫	♩ 𝄽
Beat (drums):	♩ ♩	♩ ♩

4 Create rhythmic compositions using texts

This step is the culmination of the work begun in step one. The class should then be able to combine beat and rhythm to make simple compositions. To that end, students in this step create percussion pieces with the aid of word rhythms. When a second voice is added an initial introduction to complementary rhythmic parts takes place. You might begin by suggesting the instruments but your children will very soon wish to make their own color choices.

The following verse provides a good early experience in timbre because it has a fairly interesting rhythmic construction, it contains a few words which lend themselves to color substitution, and it is short.

> Listen to the sun
> Listen to the sun
> Listen to the sun shine
> All day long.[5]

The resulting unpitched score is:

After the substitutions have been made and the rhythm is secure, the following ostinato should be taught.

Temple blocks: ♩ ♩ | ♫ ♫ :‖
Sunshine listen to the

The composition which results is:

61

Rhythm and Tonal Memory

1 Imitate movement motives in place; later in space

Obviously children must develop rhythmic memory if they are to become independent musicans. Step 1 introduces this challenge through movement activities, step 2 adds instrumentation.

Begin by asking the class to repeat a four-beat movement pattern such as tapping the head, shoulders, or thighs with both hands. Movements of the feet will lead later to such short motives in space as four walking steps (♩ ♩ ♩ ♩), two jumps (♩ ⁊ ♩ ⁊) run, run, run, run, stop, wait (♫ ♫ ♩ ⁊) and the like.

These beginnings can be developed through 'Magic Word', a favorite game of my children. Begin a movement idea (thigh-patting, for example) which the children may join when you say the magic word. Then introduce a new movement (tapping the floor, for instance) which the class may join only when you again say the magic word. Continue the movement until all are secure before introducing the next motive. Not only are your children learning to imitate movement – and laughing while doing it – but they are also going through a simple canon exercise.

2 Imitate rhythmic motives (body percussion and unpitched instruments)

The development of rhythmic memory is facilitated by echo activities. Try beginning with body-percussion rhythm patterns in four-beat units using only one sound level (usually clapping or patting) and ask the children to repeat them exactly. Older children can perform longer phrases and a mixture of body sounds.

Transfer of echo work to unpitched percussion is a greater challenge than that described above because the patterns are given in a different medium from the desired responses. You may use the four body levels (snapping, clapping, patting, and stepping) to play rhythm patterns imitated by the children on unpitched percussion instruments. For example, start by clapping a four-beat pattern which is imitated by those children holding claves and wood blocks. Begin with two groups of instruments, later adding a third, then a fourth as the children gain confidence.

Again, a game is very useful. Move to some part of the room where the children cannot see you and from this position give the body-sound cues. Interest grows if the players change instruments at regular intervals. The learning and the laughter are infectious.

3 Distinguish higher from lower pitches. Sing and locate pitches on instruments

Just as steps 1 and 2 helped children develop rhythmic memory, so steps 3 and 4 help foster tonal memory. We start this process by asking the class to distinguish high and low pitches, a distinction I delay until now so as to avoid confusion with the concepts of loud and soft. But when the time comes to present these new ideas I find that the third phrase of the singing game *Old King Glory* is very helpful in giving students the sound and feel of high and low in the voice.[6]

Old King Glory of the Mountain

My children enjoy extending the game by singing the octave tones individually around the circle. The first in turn sings 'first one', the next sings 'second one', and so on in succession until each child has sung.

Distinguishing higher from lower in smaller intervals follows the experience of the octave. The last motive of *Ring Around the Rosy* provides the descending fifth.

The descending third can be found in *Star Light, Star Bright*.

Following these experiences your children can tell on what word they hear the highest or lowest note after you have sung a new melody. Singing familiar songs twice, starting on a higher or lower pitch the second time, is another way to reinforce the concept.

Bar instruments provide a visual and aural reinforcement of the contrast between high and low. First try introducing this idea by holding the instrument vertically and playing ascending and descending patterns while the children watch, listen, and describe the sounds as moving higher or moving lower. At a later stage, have them describe the pitch movement without seeing the instrument.

The children can also use the instruments to indicate higher and lower by showing melodic movement which illustrates rhymes such as the following.[7]

<blockquote>
As I went up the apple tree
All the apples fell on me.
</blockquote>

4 Echo singing melodic motives

Echo singing is the best device I have found for developing pitch discrimination and for preparing children for later notation work. A good way to begin the mastery of these skills is with the well-known 'roll call' game. Using motives such as *s l*, *s m*, *s m d* and *m r d* sing $\overset{s\,m}{\text{'Hello}}$ $\overset{s\,m}{\text{David'}}$ and the child answers $\overset{s\,m}{\text{'Hello}}$ $\overset{s\,m}{\text{Jane'}}$. Children may then sing to one another around the circle using the descending minor third interval. Or you may sing $\overset{s\quad s\quad l}{\text{'How are you?'}}$ with the children answering $\overset{s\quad s\quad l}{\text{'I am fine'}}$ or (perhaps) $\overset{s\quad s\quad l}{\text{'I am tired'}}$. Or try $\overset{d\quad r\quad m}{\text{'Can you run?'}}$ with your class replying $\overset{d\quad r\quad m}{\text{'I can run'}}$. My children love the opportunity to sing questions for me to answer. If I sing back too low or too high, the class must help identify the problem and help me to sing the interval at the correct pitch. Needless to say, they especially love this part of the game.

If you wish to isolate a particular melodic motive in a new song, sing it on a neutral syllable and have the class echo. Then ask the class to find the motive as you sing the entire song with text.

Rhythm Notation

1 Read, clap, play ♩ ♫ 𝄽

By this time most students have had enough musical experience to begin comprehending notation. Hence, in this and the next two steps they will learn to read and write rhythm symbols.

Beat (♩) and its division (♫) are the first note values to be presented in symbols to your students. I like to start as simply as possible by introducing only the beat symbol first. I next ask the class to speak, then clap the *Minnesota* rhyme learned earlier. Then present the rhyme in its symbol form.

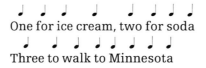

One for ice cream, two for soda
Three to walk to Minnesota

Now as we turn to the notation of eighth notes and the quarter rest we again make use of all media (speech, song, movement, and instruments) to enhance the likelihood that students will understand and retain these ideas.

Speech. Here is another rhyme game that furnishes an effective means of introducing the division of the beat and the quarter rest.

♩ ♫ ♩ ♫ ♩ ♫ ♩ 𝄽   ♩ ♫ ♩ ♫ ♫ ♫ ♩ 𝄽
One color two color three color four   Five color six color seven color more

Have the class speak the rhyme, then speak the rhyme and clap the rhythm of the words. The rest (𝄽) is indicated by separated hands, palms up. Half of the children pat the beat, half text rhythm, then reverse the tasks. Now ask the students if the claps and beats were exactly alike. When children describe the faster motion on the words 'color' and 'seven' you should introduce the symbol ♫. Also present the symbol for no sound (𝄽) at this time.

Children arranged in a seated circle are now ready to experience the flow of the beat. As you point to each student in succession, that child speaks two beats of the rhyme. For example, the first child says 'One color', the second says 'two colors', and so on until the fourth child stands on 'four'. Continue around the circle until all are standing. A considerably more challenging version of this game involves saying the words consecutively around the circle at *one*-beat intervals.

Cards might be distributed on which ♩ and ♫ are printed. Eight children (each designated as a beat) are selected to hold the cards while the class speaks, then claps the rhythm of the symbols arranged as follows: ♩ ♫ ♩ ♫ ♩ ♫ ♩ 𝄽. Now reverse the note values (♫ ♩) but keep the rest constant to indicate the end of the phrase. Many teachers select from a number of systems those rhythm syllables which they decide are most effective in building reading skills with children. Two popular choices are 'ta' (♩) and 'ti ti' (♫) and the use of 'tah, tah, teh' to describe ♩ ♫.

A particularly graphic illustration of the beat concept can be achieved by using four chairs to represent beats. Invite four children, each of whom depicts a quarter note, to fill these chairs, and the class claps the pattern. Removing one child, leaving an empty chair, creates a rest (𝄽). The real fun begins when two children (♫) are invited to share one of the chairs in the sequence. My children greatly enjoy clapping a variety of different four-beat patterns using their classmates as quarter- and eighth-note representatives.

Song. One, Two, Tie My Shoe offers a familiar arrangement of ♩ and ♫. After the song has been sung several times, the children are ready to determine the number of sounds per beat and to notate the first four beats in rhythm symbols.

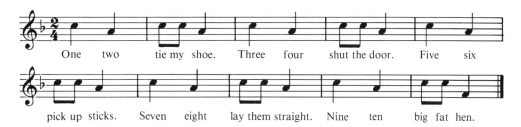

One two   tie my shoe.   Three   four   shut the door.   Five   six

pick up sticks.   Seven   eight   lay them straight.   Nine   ten   big fat hen.

Movement. I find that simple movement activity helps to reinforce the concept of the division of the beat. One half of the group is invited to take two steps as they sing 'One two'; the other half answers by clapping the rhythm of the words while singing 'tie my shoe'. Repeat until the song is finished. Be certain to reverse the tasks so that all children have the movement experience. Also ask the class to write the two steps (♩ ♩) and the clapped rhythm (♫♩) in notation symbols.

Instruments. Try one unpitched instrument for 'One, two' and a contrasting color for 'tie my shoe' to explore ♩ and ♫ a different way. A new game offers further reinforcement. Seat your students in a circle and distribute hand drums and claves among them. Instruct those with drums to play quarter notes, those with claves to play eighth notes. While you keep the beat at the piano or on temple blocks, the children play the note values dictated by their instrument. Clustering the instruments rather than alternating drums and claves will create a more interesting result.

Improvisation. Children who are secure with pitch and rhythm patterns can use them to invent new material. An appropriate example might be to ask the children to think four beats, then substitute any combination of eighths and quarters for two of the four. They ought to show the two silent beats as they have learned to demonstrate the rest. Now ask the remainder of the class to provide one sound for each of the improviser's two silent beats. Finally, put two different patterns together to be imitated by the rest of the class to experience a longer phrase.

2 Identify ‖, :‖ and ostinato
My children usually grasp the concept of :‖ very easily when it is introduced in a familiar context. You might begin by reviewing *One Two* (♩ ♩ ♫♩); then explain that :‖ saves the trouble of writing out the pattern five times.

The difference between :‖ and ‖ can be taught immediately. Review ♩ ♩ ♫♩ now followed by ‖. The children must stop at the end of the four beats. To test for comprehension ask your class to read a new rhythmic phrase: ♩ ♩ :‖ ♩ ♫ ‖ ♩ 𝄽 ‖.

Half of the group claps the rhythmic phrase, the other half pats ♩ 𝄽 :‖. This repeated pattern is identified as an ostinato.

3 Create one, then two voice rhythm pieces using ♩ ♫ 𝄽
Children love to make new arrangements of the notation symbols they have learned. A first step involves locating ♫ on the first, second, or third beats of a four-beat phrase; ♫ may then be tried on two, followed by three of the four beats. Each new combination must be performed accurately before proceeding to the next step. The children will discover for themselves that ♩ is a more appropriate phrase ending than ♫.

Now ask your class to read and then to add a new combination of four beats to the first motive. Have them speak, then clap the resulting eight-beat phrase and transfer it to claves or hand drums. An ostinato (♩ 𝄽) which the children will remember from an earlier piece is added to create a two-voice texture.

66

This ostinato should be performed on an instrument which complements the color of the first rhythmic phrase. The resulting score might be:

Accompaniment

1 Perform the beat simultaneously with a spoken text

When your children can do two musical tasks simultaneously they are in fact accompanying themselves. In this step we do that by combining a spoken text with a beat. Of course, the class must by now be able to respond to an external beat by patting, clapping, and stepping it accurately. A review of *One, Two, Tie My Shoe* offers you the opportunity to work with a four-beat unit involving only one beat of ♫. Students begin by speaking 'One, two, three, four', while patting their thighs. They stop speaking while continuing to pat the beat. The text of the rhyme is added when all are secure. The beat should be played on the floor, by clapping, by stepping in place, and, finally, by stepping in space. The need for moving carefully from one of these responses to the next cannot be overemphasized.

After the children have mastered saying and playing the beats in units of four, they are ready for the extension to an eight-beat phrase. *Jean, Jean* is one of hundreds of jump-rope rhymes and jingles which can be used for this purpose.

Jean, Jean, dress'd in green, Went downtown to eat ice cream.

One group of students chants 'ice cream', (♩ ♩) to establish beat security, while the other speaks the rhyme. The beat is then performed by first patting, then clapping, and finally stepping while the words are spoken. A significantly more complicated challenge for older children involves clapping the word rhythms while stepping the beat.

2 Sing melody and play the beat simultaneously

The same steps outlined in the preceding paragraph apply to this activity, with the exception that the words are sung, not spoken. After the class has sung *One, Two, Tie My Shoe* while patting, clapping, and stepping the beat, invite the children to perform the beat in a similar fashion with other familiar songs.

3 Add a simple tonic accompaniment to appropriate melodies

The first use of bar instruments for accompaniment purposes is based on one note only. This pedal point on the tonic in the bass can be performed as a tremolo or sounded on the strong beats of the melody. These two ideas are combined in the following example.

I See the Moon

JF

I see the moon and the moon sees ___ me.

God bless the moon and ___ God bless ___ me.

* Play on any notes in G pentatonic; change notes on each beat.

4 Accompany appropriate song material with simple bordun played on bar instruments as a chord on strong beats

Most students find it very easy to transfer beats from their thighs to bar instruments. Beginning with the familiar, the children sing *One, Two*, adding the beat patted on their thighs. Then ask them to pat one beat, rest one beat as they sing the song. This pattern (♩) is transferred to the bass xylophone with bars removed to facilitate accuracy.

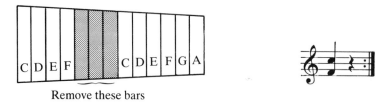

Remove these bars

Bordun patterns for other pentatonic songs can be prepared exactly as outlined above.

5 Accompany appropriate song material with level bordun

The level bordun is merely a chord bordun in alternating registers. It may be performed on one or more instruments, but care must be taken to keep the tonic below the voice parts on the strong beats. The following example illustrates two of its typical functions: to add color to an orchestration and to create tension in the phrase.

Star Light, Star Bright

Trad./arr. JF

6 Add a second complementary sound color to bordun accompaniment for songs

The first sound color to be added to the voice and simple bordun will be an unpitched instrument. The rhythm of this part should complement, not imitate, the voice and bordun rhythms. When we add a complementary sound color to *One, Two* (p.68) the resulting rhythmic texture looks like this:

melodic rhythm
complementary sound color (woodblock, hand drum)
BX bordun rhythm

In the following example, both glockenspiels and finger cymbals are added for color.

Sally Over the Water

Georgia/arr. JF

Sal – ly o – ver the wa – ter, Sal – ly o –ver the sea,

Sal – ly catch a black – bird, can't catch me!

*7 Accompany song material with broken bordun accompaniment.
A second complementary sound color and/or an unpitched
percussion part may be added*

Playing one bordun tone after another is a natural step for children to take following the playing of two tones together. A small chart illustrates that this new pattern begins with the left hand.

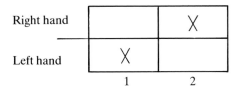

Be sure to proceed slowly at first since the broken bordun requires alternating arm movements and hence is more difficult to perform accurately than the chord bordun.

The setting of the pentatonic song *Bluebird* uses the broken and chord borduns in a complementary rhythmic style.

Bluebird

American/arr. JF

71

Melody

1 Imitate, then improvise melodies vocally and on instruments using the mi re do *motive. Add a simple tonic accompaniment*

Grade One is a vocabulary building year. At this level children are introduced to melodic patterns which they imitate and upon which they improvise. These motives, sung and played on instruments, provide a pentatonic vocabulary which will be notated on a staff in Grade Two.

The *m r d* motive , which children have been hearing in a variety of ways since the beginning of the year, is made conscious by singing *Down Came a Lady*.

Down Came a Lady

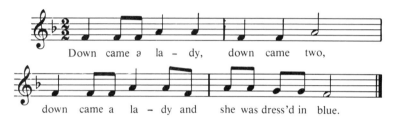

After the children have learned the song, individuals take turns singing to one another on the first three phrases. All the children sing 'she was dressed in blue'; you later identify these sounds as *m m r d*.

Locating these pitches on an instrument is the next step. Ask the children to find their biggest bar (low C) and name it *do*. They will quickly discover how to play *m r d*. You can reinforce the idea of the descending pitch pattern by holding the instrument in front of the children in vertical fashion as you play *m r d* for them.

Now ask the class to sing *Hot Cross Buns*. Can they locate the *m r d* motive on C *do*? On G *do*? Next ask that they substitute Orff instruments for the singing whenever *m r d* appears in the song. They may first sing, then think the 'one a-penny' section. Patting the four beats of this motive helps the class maintain the tempo. To create an instrumental piece, you may add the tonic note on a bass instrument while xylophones or metallophones play *m r d*. Temple block, wood block or claves may be substituted for 'one a-penny'.

Hot Cross Buns

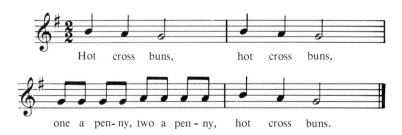

Ask them to find the *m r d* motive in such other favorite songs as *Three Blind Mice*, and *Old King Glory*.

The children are now ready to begin making up their own little melodies using the motive they have learned. Ask them to see how many different ways they can sing the three pitches. In order to remember their ideas, you will write ♩♩♩ *r m d* or ♩♩♩ *d r m* or whatever order they contribute. You may want to notate these patterns as illustrated above on a large sheet of paper and sign each contributor's name for later class practice. When you are satisfied that the children feel comfortable singing the three pitches with syllables in different orders, ask them to create a *m r d* melody for the rhyme:

> Would you have a dream come true? (singer 1)
> Tell it one but never two (singer 2)

The first singer may use only *m* and *r* pitches, the second only *r* and *d*, ending on *d*. *M r d* improvisations can be encouraged on the bar instruments by asking three children to play four beats each in succession (ask them to repeat one note and to avoid ending on *do*) and a fourth to play *m r d*. Basses can support by playing half notes on the tonic. In this way we are beginning to explore phrase structure and form with only three notes.

2 Play aural recognition games using the mi re do syllables

After the children have much practice in singing and playing the *m r d* pattern you will want to test their tonal memory using the three pitches. It is important to approach this activity as a game using both vocal and instrumental responses because I've found that some children who are not yet confident singers can play patterns accurately on instruments.

You may give the cue vocally, on a tenor recorder, or alto xylophone. Note that the instruments selected are pitched in the child's vocal range. I find it works best to start on the same note, say *mi*, for each pattern and to give vocal cues on a neutral syllable such as loo. The procedure is:

teacher sings

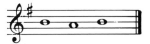

child echoes
vocally on tone syllables
or on alto xylophone

In the initial stages, mistakes are accepted in the same way as accurate responses. As the children become familiar with the game, the class can sing the correct syllable response if a mistake is made. However, it is very important to create a comfortable atmosphere so that mistakes are accepted as an inevitable part of the learning process. My approach is to select a very able student to take my place; when I err in responding I ask the class to help me. Such an example invariably minimizes embarrassment and maximizes cooperation.

When the children are familiar with imitating patterns on instruments, invite two children to play the alto xylophones. You give the motive to the first; if she succeeds she chooses someone else in the circle to take her place at the instrument while you are giving a new motive to the second player. If she makes a mistake, ask the second child for help and give the first another chance to succeed.

3 Add tone syllable names to rhythm syllables as a step toward music reading

After the children have had much practice with three-tone (*m r d*) and three-rhythm (♩ ♫ 𝄾) patterns, they enjoy the challenge of playing musical detective; that is, deciphering songs they know from notation. Ask them to identify *Down Came a Lady* written as follows:

Another day try:

Finally, your class will be ready to teach themselves a new melody:

Didn't old Noah build the ark?
Built it out of hickory bark.

In came the animals two by two,
Hippopotamus and Kangaroo.

In came the animals three by three,
Two big cats and a bumblebee.

In came the animals four by four,
Two through the window and two through the door.

In came the animals five by five,
Four with sparrows and the redbird's wife.

In came the animals six by six,
Elephant laughed at the monkey's tricks.

In came the animals seven by seven,
Four from home and the rest from heaven.

In came the animals eight by eight,
Some were on time and the others were late.

In came the animals nine by nine,
Some were shouting and some were crying.

In came the animals ten by ten,
Five black roosters and five black hens.

Now Noah says, go shut that door,
The rain's started dropping and we can't take more.

When the children have had several experiences recognizing familiar melodies and reading new ones they will want to try to use this new skill to remember what they create for themselves. This activity was introduced in step 2; we now ask the class to help notate individual improvised four-beat *m r d* melodies. The children are always eager to play their new melodies on bar instruments; through this means the children become aware that the function of notation is to assure that no one's melody will be forgotten.

4 Introduce sol *and* la *pitches to complete the pentatonic scale vocabulary. Identify specific intervals from this scale isolated from song literature; add tonic and bordun accompaniments*

The introduction to the pentatonic scale is completed by adding pitches to the *m r d* motive which the children learned in steps 1 and 2. *Sol* is introduced in a lullaby, first sung then played on bar instruments over a level bordun accompaniment.

Lullaby

Trad./arr. JF

Go to sleep my lit – tle ba – by, go to sleep and do not cry.

You might sing the melody on loo and ask the children to join you when they hear the *d r m* motive. Identify the new pitch as *sol*, and sing the entire melody with syllables. The children will discover that they must skip a note between *mi* and *sol* when they try it out on the bar instruments.

S m r d is reinforced in the second phrase of *Jim Along Josie*.

75

Jim Along Josie

American/arr. JF

The accompaniment for *Josie* also works well for *Mary Had a Little Lamb*. A change of color (from glockenspiel to triangle) played on the first beat of the second and fourth measures is all that is necessary to enhance the melody. The interval *mi* to *sol* can be practiced in *Mary*.

Mary Had a Little Lamb

This is a good time to review *One, Two, Tie My Shoe* now sung with syllables and, perhaps, transferred to bar instruments.

Bounce High introduces the syllable *la*. Ask the children to locate the pattern ♩♩♩♩ on their instruments after they sing it with syllables.

s l s m

Your children will remember that there are three steps in the *sol-mi* interval; the major second between *sol* and *la* is now visually reinforced. The accompaniment provides a reinforcement of the text references to high and low.

Bounce High

arr. JF

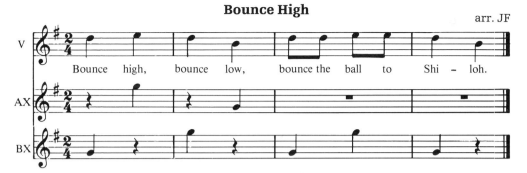

After the children have learned to sing *Lucy Locket* by rote, ask them to try to sing it with syllables.

Notate the first motive: ♩♩♩♩♩♩ *s s l l s s m m*. Now substitute the text for all but the second beat of the pattern. The children are delighted to discover that Lucy's and Kitty's last names have been changed to 'La La'. Vocal or instrumental improvisation can be facilitated by singing or playing the text 'absent-minded Lucy' on *s*, *m*, and/or *l*. Here is a full score of *Lucy Locket* for those of you who might wish to develop this material still further.

Lucy Locket

Trad./arr. JF

77

The *Bluebird* melody was first taught by rote on page 71. Now the children can sing the melodic outline from syllables.

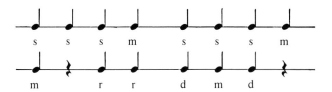

If you want to play the game at this point, choose a bluebird who walks in and out the windows formed by a circle of children holding hands. The bluebird claps a partner's hands four times on 'hi, diddle um day, day, day'. The second verse is:

> Takes himself a partner
> Walks in the garden,
> Hi, diddle um
> Day, day, day.

The bluebird and his partner go walking until 'high diddle' when he returns to the circle leaving the new bluebird to resume the game.

The pattern *s m d* is reinforced in *Bought Me a Cat*. This song, a favorite of children, may be accompanied by a broken bordun as indicated here.

Bought Me a Cat

American/arr. JF

2. Hen went "chim-mey chuck"
3. Goose went "qua qua"
4. Cow went "moo moo"

Finally, *Ring Around the Rosy* provides the *s d* pattern. The orchestration uses the same notes in a level bordun and in the glockenspiel color part. Children are fascinated by such connections between melody and accompaniment.

Ring Around the Rosy

Listening

Sing, play, and listen to music in binary (AB) form

Helping children to make connections between the music which they can make for themselves and art music beyond their performance capabilities is a prerequisite to active listening. If your students are given a specific listening task, another aspect of musical behavior becomes functional for them. That is why it is important to give the class many opportunities to listen to examples of the use of expressive elements in art music throughout the year. Exploration of musical form, however, is delayed until this point because it is a more abstract concept.

Ducks in the Millpond provides a clear example of a melody in binary form. Divide the group, giving each half the responsibility for performing one section of the song. Compare the rhythms of the song and the length of the A and B sections to those of the percussion piece.

Ducks in the Millpond

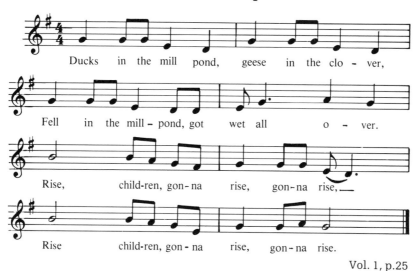

Ducks in the mill pond, geese in the clo - ver,

Fell in the mill - pond, got wet all o - ver.

Rise, child-ren, gon-na rise, gon-na rise, —

Rise child-ren, gon - na rise, gon - na rise.

Vol. 1, p.25

Percussion Piece

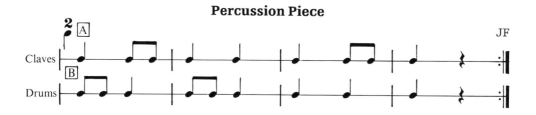

JF

Claves

Drums

These preliminary activities should have prepared the children's ears for the Bach Menuet from the *Notebook for Anna Magdalena Bach* (1725), which provides a clear example of two-part form. Although the children have practiced listening to short phrases, they will need encouragement to extend

Menuet from the Notebook for Anna Magdalena Bach

J S Bach

Gavotte from French Suite No. 5

J S Bach

their attention to an entire section to determine the number of full stops in the composition. Movement will help the students to identify the differences between the sections. Ask them to locate the four appearances of the two-measure beginning motive: ♩ ♫ ♫ | ♩ ♩ ♩. They will step, step, step, step, clap, clap on this motive; turn with a partner on measures 5-8 and 13-16. The students turn the first four measures of the B section as they did in the second phrase of A, clapping the beat on the four measures which follow. The last eight measures of the B section are a repeat of the first eight. Dividing the children into two groups visually reinforces the two-part form of this piece.

A more challenging example of this form is to be found in the Gavotte from the Bach French Suite #V. The students should be encouraged to listen for the different lengths of the A and B sections, the reverse melodic direction of the first motive in the B section, and the increased rhythmic activity in the B section.

6 · Grade Two: Beyond the First Steps

Your first-level students learned some of the rudiments of music through singing and speaking, moving and playing. Now, with some awareness of pitch and rhythm, they are ready for the following six objectives.

1. To further develop rhythmic competencies. We begin with augmentation of the beat. As you will recall, your students learned its division in Grade One; now they will read and write the resulting half note and its equivalent rest after much aural experience. When your class has had sufficient practice performing the beat, its division and its augmentation, the students will be ready to group these different note values into meter. Now the class is ready for the challenge of developing musical independence provided by rhythm canons. When your students have mastered these difficulties they are ready to create little pieces of their own with evaluation following. The last rhythmic challenge is teaching children to perform two different tasks simultaneously. Obviously, the range of musical responses would be limited without this skill so the earlier we begin its mastery the better.

2. To notate the five-tone scale. In the first year your students had considerable experience singing and playing pentatonic pieces; now they learn the pitch symbols. This essential skill not only enables children to have a record of their own compositions but to learn new music for themselves, including that of their classmates. Mastery of the pentatonic has a number of advantages. Students find it easier to improvise because of the absence of harmonic implications. Second, there are fewer intervals to master than in diatonic. Lastly, your class will gain access to America's rich folk music heritage, much of which is in the pentatonic.

3. To encourage improvisation. This is done through exercises that give increasing creative responsibilities to the child. In these activities the class works with rhythm provided by a text, rhythm developed through phrase building, and three-note melodies.

4. To foster the student's musical independence by introducing rudimentary counterpoint in both melody and rhythm. Children, of course, need to learn to maintain their own parts against others in a group; as with all else in this grade, it is a skill fundamental to their progress.

5. To build on the rhythmic competencies learned earlier in the year (augmenting the beat and arranging rhythm into two-beat units). Now the class is introduced to a four-fold extension of the beat (⋅⋅), $\frac{4}{4}$ meter and eight, rather than four-beat rhythmic phrases. These more complex rhythmic challenges are delayed to this point so as to provide students with many

opportunities to master fully the rhythmic material introduced at the beginning of the year.

6. In a listening exercise, your students apply the vocabulary and concepts learned this year to music they are not able to perform. This experience enables the class to begin understanding music at a new level of complexity. In the process, they are reminded of a point first made at the end of Grade One: their own musical efforts are part of a larger musical world.

Here are the goals and the steps designed to accomplish them.

Rhythm I

1 Introduce the half note by adding a tie to two quarters: ♩ ♩ = ♩
2 Define $\frac{2}{4}$ meter. Determine bar-line placement for rhymes and rhythm patterns in $\frac{2}{4}$
3 Perform movement, speech, and rhythm canons (overlapping imitation)
4 Read, write, and perform ♩ and ‑ in songs, rhythm and instrumental pieces
5 Create rhythm pieces using ♫ ♩ ♩ ♩ ‖ ‑ . Add one complementary ostinato
6 Take simple rhythmic dictation (four-beat units)
7 Clap rhythm of songs and rhymes while walking the beat
8 Clap a simple complementary ostinato while singing

Melody Notation

1 Review *mi re do* motive. Locate on the staff; sing and play on bar instruments
2 Review *sol mi do* and *mi sol la* motives. Locate on the staff; sing and play on bar instruments
3 Accompany *m r d* songs with moving bordun (two players). A complementary sound color or ostinato may be added
4 Read, write, sing, and play songs in pentatonic (F and G tonal centers)

Improvisation

1 Use texts as basis for rhythmic exploration on pitched and unpitched instruments
2 Build rhythmic phrases using four-beat questions and answers performed with unpitched or body percussion
3 Vocally improvise a short rhyme using *m r d* motive
4 Improvise questions and answers on bar instruments using *m r d* motive

Texture: Counterpoint

1 Perform speech, movement, body, and unpitched percussion ostinati as accompaniments to texts (one or two accompaniment voices)
2 Perform vocal ostinati as accompaniments to pentatonic melodies
3 Learn simple two-part rhythm canons
4 Learn simple two-part melodic canons

Rhythm II

1 Identify ○ as ♩ ♩ ♩ ♩ and ♩ ♩
2 Read, write, perform ○ and ▬ in melody and rhythm pieces
3 Define $\frac{4}{4}$ meter. Determine bar-line placement for rhymes and rhythm patterns in $\frac{4}{4}$
4 Construct eight-beat rhythmic phrases using ♫ ♩ ♩ ♪ ▬ ○ ▬. Add one or two accompanying ostinato parts of varying lengths

Listening

1 Perform and listen to ABA form

Rhythm 1

1 Introduce the half note by adding a tie to two quarter notes: ♩ ♩ = ♩

Your children's first experience of augmentation of the beat will be the half note. As is frequently the case in Orff instruction, movement provides the opportunity to feel this duration before the symbol is encountered. First, have the students walk to the beat of a drum, then have them walk and clap the beat simultaneously.

To establish the feeling of a two-beat unit, have your class step the beat but clap only every other beat. When they are comfortable with this activity, the new challenge of clapping the first and holding second beat may be presented. But remember that clapping ♩ is a more difficult task for young children than clapping ♩ ♪. At a prearranged signal ask the children to alternate clapping quarter and half notes.

The symbol of the half note is best presented after you have explained the idea of a two-beat unit. First show the children: ♩ ♩ and then tie the notes together: ♩ ♩. After erasing the bow, point out that ♩ = ♩ ♩. Now your class should be prepared to play all sorts of notation games. A favorite initial approach at my school is to use a grid which illustrates various rhythmic combinations within a four-beat framework. Here are some possibilities.

After your students have clapped these patterns they are ready to create their own patterns on a grid. These little four-beat phrases may be clapped or performed on percussion instruments. Finally, the students should transfer the grid patterns to conventional notation and perform them.

2 Define $\frac{2}{4}$ meter. Determine bar-line placement for rhymes and rhythm patterns in $\frac{2}{4}$

A little rhyme provides the initial activity for this concept. Children say ♩ ♩ Tic tac ♩ ♩ toe, round I go first clapping, then stepping the note values while speaking the rhyme. A lively little game can now be developed from this text. Children step quarters and clap the half notes. Next ask the students to pair off. Partners step the first two beats and clap one another's hands on ♩ . An unpitched percussion accompaniment helps define this movement pattern.

Hanging cymbal
Drum

Ask the children to help you notate the rhyme they have just performed. Add an accent mark under the stressed words as an introduction to metric accent.

♩ ♪ ♩ ♩ ♪ ♩
\>　　\>　\>　　\>

Substitute bar lines for accent marks and indicate the metric grouping with the sign $\frac{2}{\curvearrowright}$. After you've explained that the number indicates *how many* beats and the symbol illustrates *what sort* of note receives one beat, substitute the $\frac{2}{4}$ meter signature for $\frac{2}{\curvearrowright}$. Both may be used interchangeably throughout the elementary school years.

Invite the students to locate metric accents in other songs and rhymes which they know.

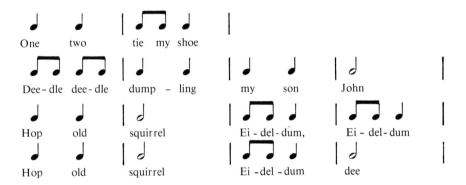

Patting the metric accent while performing the songs and rhymes gives the sense of strong-weak and turns your young performers into conductors. Stepping *only* the metric accent while singing or speaking is a related activity which gives further practice in $\frac{2}{4}$ meter.

3 Perform movement, speech, and rhythm canons (overlapping imitation)

The concept of overlapping parts can be introduced to children through a game based on the 'Simon says' idea. The class agrees on a magic word which, when spoken, indicates that the class is to follow your movement. The game begins when you make some simple gesture such as clapping. The class will also clap when the magic word is spoken. Once this is mastered you can proceed to a new movement idea (such as turning in place, patting the floor, patting your head, and the like); soon you can invite the children to join by speaking the magic word. The musical challenge results from concentrating on learning a new activity while performing a familiar one.

Another kind of canon movement activity is inspired by a text. Children first learn the poem which they later accompany with appropriate movement and, possibly, body percussion color. The piece is then performed by two groups in canon and, finally, the movement is performed in canon without the text. Here is an example.

1 Ordinary clapsies,
(Clap hands on beat)

2 Rolypoly backsies,
(Hands circle around one another)

3 High, low,
(Snap high, snap low)

4 The heel and the toe
(Extend right heel, cross R toe over L foot)

5 Clip, clop
(Pat thighs on beat)

6 And away we go!
(Step step step)

A text can also be used to develop the rhythmic security so essential to contrapuntal singing. The familiar 'Star light, star bright, first star I see tonight' lends itself nicely to canon exploration. I have my children speak all the words in unison, then in canon (group two begins when group one has reached the word 'first'). The real fun begins when certain words are spoken while others are internalized. For example, the students may be asked to speak only the underlined words in unison.

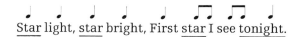
Star light, star bright, First star I see tonight.

The canon may now be performed using only underlined words. Substituting unpitched color (such as a triangle and drum) for the underlined words is an interesting extension of this idea.

Rhythmic notation provides yet another means of exploring overlapping parts. The children begin by reading the following rhythm at sight.

When the rhythm is secure, body percussion colors can be assigned to identify note values; for instance, quarter notes might be clapped while eighth notes are patted on thighs. The rhythmic motives and colors are nicely complementary if the canon is begun at the second measure.

4 *Read, write, perform ♩ and ▬ in songs, rhythm, and instrumental pieces*

Song. Page's Train, introduced in Chapter Four, offers an opportunity to explore the half note three times in the melody. Because it is found at the ends of phrases, care must be taken to give the note its full value. Call the children's attention to the supporting level bordun and point out that the metallophone sustains half notes because of its resonance.

Page's Train

American/arr. JF

Another melody for half-note exploration is *Down the Road*. If the tune is presented with rhythmic accuracy the students can discover the half notes for themselves. This is accomplished by singing the melody while patting the beat, then internalizing all melody tones except 'road' (the half notes) which they sing out loud.

Down the road, down the road,

Come a - long let's walk to - ge - ther, down the road.

Rhythm Piece. The melodic rhythm *Who's That?* provides the chance to practice the half note in relationship to both eighth and quarter notes.

Who's that tap-ping at the win – dow?

Who's that knock-ing at the door?

After this song is part of your children's repertoire, you may later want to test their rhythmic memories by putting the rhythm notation on the board. When the song has been correctly identified, the note values can be transferred to unpitched instruments as illustrated in the following score. I've added a hand drum ostinato because I find it provides needed rhythmic security for the performers.

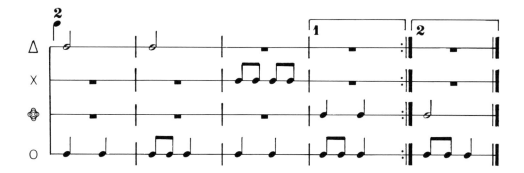

Instrumental Piece. Students encounter ♩ and ₋ in the glockenspiel and cymbal parts of this little piece. Try having the class say 'clap-hold' and 'rest-hold' as they all practice the glockenspiel part. This helps the players perform the part correctly. The cymbal part echoes this rhythm in the B section.

90

Instrumental Piece

Give the students papers which are divided into sections; ask them to notate the glockenspiel and bass metallophone parts. The results will be:

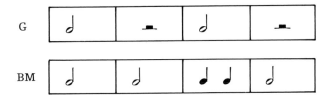

5 Create rhythm pieces using ♫ ♩ ♩ ♪ 𝄽 ＿. Add one complementary ostinato

The following model is an example of a two-voice composition for body or unpitched percussion instruments. Several ostinato possibilities are provided.

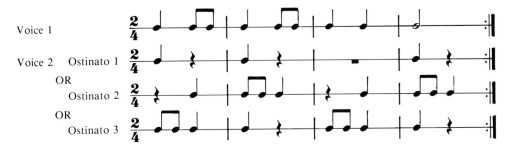

This is also a good time to have the children work cooperatively to create percussion compositions. Ask each group of students to construct four measures to be followed by a performance for the class. You may add a second voice ostinato to the original composition with each group then assigned to play an ostinato accompaniment for another's original piece.

6 Take simple rhythmic dictation (four-beat units)

Orff teachers have come to recognize that evaluation is a critical part of child-centered music learning. While observation of skill mastery is the most typical evaluation device, a more precise approach is the short dictation test which I make more palatable by calling the 'big ears game' (as in 'what big ears you must have to remember all these rhythms'). But, by whatever name, it provides a quick, effective means of assessing student comprehension of rhythmic material.

Rhythmic dictation can be expedited by providing a simple form on which the children can write the rhythms you clap for them. Since four examples of four beats are sufficient at this point, the form might look something like this (each square represents one beat).

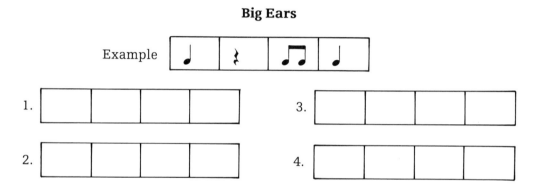

The following rhythms illustrate examples appropriate for this level.

My children enjoy using the dictation exercise as an opportunity to create their own little four-beat patterns. This works well when one child claps his own rhythm while another notates it on the board. The class together then solves the notation or performance problems that may arise.

7 Clap rhythm of songs and rhymes while walking the beat

This skill promotes rhythmic security but it must be handled very carefully when first introduced to the children. You will soon observe that it is easier for your class to clap rhythms which are faster than the beat and so, at first, you will want to introduce examples like the following.

Aca baca soda cracker, Aca baca boo

Aca baca soda cracker, Out goes you!

Two songs very appropriate for practicing the skill during this introductory stage are *Let us Chase the Squirrel* (♫ ♫♩ ♩) and *Bingo* (♪| ♫ ♫ ♫ ♫ | ♫ ♫♩ ♩). Invite the children to suggest other examples.

8 *Clap a simple complementary ostinato while singing*

You have laid the groundwork for simultaneous performance of two contrasting parts in the previous activity. This new challenge, however, requires the ability to play a rhythmic part which is complementary to the melody. I find that children are greatly helped by making sure the ostinato is secure before the melody is added. A moderate tempo will also aid success. After the two parts have been mastered, some of your students may want to attempt yet another challenge: stepping the beat as they clap the ostinato and sing the melody.

Sailor

A sail-or went to sea, to see what he could see, and all that he could see was the deep blue sea.

Who's That?

Who's that tap-ping at the win - dow?

Who's that knock-ing at the door?

Down the Road

Down the road, down the road, come a-long let's walk to-ge-ther, down the road.

Melody Notation

1 Review mi re do *and* sol mi la *motives. Locate on the staff; sing and play on bar instruments*

In my experience, the introduction of staff notation is best delayed until children have had much practice singing, playing, and improvising melodies using intervals from the pentatonic scale. Now that this vocabulary is familiar, they are ready to learn the symbols which represent these sounds. We will explore these challenges in this and the next two steps.

Students like to begin notation work by making notes (•) on lines and in spaces on the staff at random. This freedom provides a good opportunity to clarify the term 'on a line'. This is confusing for young children because they have learned that 'on' means to place on top of: ﻭ . Children greatly enjoy practicing the musical use of the term; to refine the task ask them to draw one stave of notes on lines and another on spaces. Then ask them to try a whole stave of notes on the same line or in the same space. In order to impress upon students the fact that notes symbolize pitch, perform a child's paper by singing or playing it on a melody instrument.

Now your class is ready for more specific notation challenges. Review the *m r d* motive by playing it on an alto xylophone. 'Did I skip any bars? Did I go up or down? Do you know a song that sounds like that?' are the kinds of questions which will prepare them for the notation work to follow.

Many children don't understand the idea of a linear progression of notes unless you help them by defining spaces in which they can write. For this reason I supply paper ruled as follows.

Let the class choose a line or space to serve as *do*. Mark it in some significant way (with an x or →) and write a note in it. (I use whole notes without reference to duration.) Now ask your students to write *re* in the next box, then

94

mi and then to sing the three notes they have written. Skip the next box, but reverse the notes in the following three writing *m r d*. When they sing these notes they are delighted to discover that they've written the first part of *Hot Cross Buns*. In subsequent lessons ask the children to write such other songs from first grade as *Didn't Old Noah?* and *Down Came a Lady*.

After providing many opportunities to write *m r d* motives from familiar song literature, you will want to see whether children can sing a new melody at sight. Ask the children to sing the first note of the following melody after you've sung *do*.

Now ask them to sing the syllables from the score. To introduce the first two phrases of *Tideo* you should sing *sols* after the students sing *mi* in measures one, two, and three. Add these *sols* to the score and ask the children to sing the entire melody.

Finally, ask one child at a time to sing pattern one, two, three or four.

At this point, I suggest that you teach the text of *Tideo*. Learn the last phrase (see overleaf) by rote with instrumental parts added to this A section melody. Although word cues are helpful to the players, counting beats and rests is a better musical approach to learning the SX and SG parts in this score. For instance, you may say, 'Glockenspiels play only on the word *pass*,' but your students will grow in independence by being asked to play the first beat in a set of four (three times). The B section melody should be added later; care must be taken to call attention to the color change in the accompaniment which emphasizes the form. Note that *do* has been relocated in the following score.

You can make good use of instruments to help reinforce pitch location. Ask one group of players (glockenspiels, for instance) to play the *m s s* motive; the xylophones to play *m r d*.

A bit of improvisation also adds to the fun. Try using the *Tideo* word rhythms and *s l m* and *m r d* motives in a variety of new ways suggested by the students. The following example represents the kind of new piece which might result.

95

Tideo

American/arr. JF

2 Review sol mi do *and* mi sol la *motives. Locate on the staff; sing and play on bar instruments*

After your class has learned to sing *What'll We Do With the Baby?*, you may isolate the *sol mi do* motive which appears in the second measure by notating it on a staff.

The children can then be asked to discover other ways of singing these three pitches while keeping the rhythm constant. The possibilities should be notated on a staff.

Change measure five above to ♩ ♩ ♩ (s m) and play every other measure on the glockenspiel as indicated in the score. The bass part may be presented in two sets of four beats ♩ ♩ ♩ ▪ | ♩ ♩ ♩ ▪ | (F F F   C C F).

What'll We Do with the Baby?

American/arr. JF

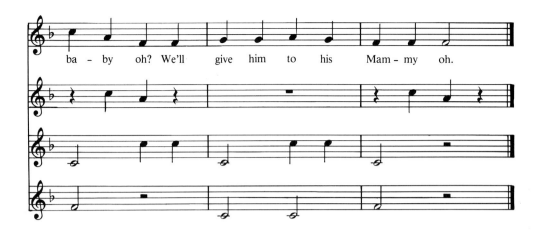

2. We'll swing him high and swing him low.
3. We'll rock him in his cradle oh.

We all know that applying notation skills to unfamiliar material is a good test of understanding. The first phrase of *Built My Lady* offers a review of the *m s l* motive and the *s m d* pattern. Because it is a good idea to review all of the relevant pitches before undertaking any sight-singing examples, you or a child may direct the singing of the now familiar pentatonic pitches.

l

s

m

r

d

The new example is then sung first silently, then aloud.

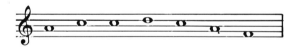

Bar instruments may be substituted for voices to emphasize the *s m d* motive; other motives may be added until the entire melody is performed on contrasting instruments. The complementary clapped ostinato may be transferred to an unpitched percussion color.

Built My Lady

Put her in but she jumped out. Fare you well my dar – ling.

3 Accompany m r d *songs with moving bordun (two players). A complementary sound color or ostinato may be added*

The children have, by this time, become very familiar with performing the simple bordun as a chord in the bass. Preparation for the introduction of moving bordun accompaniment can be made by dividing the two tones among two instruments, ie:

Chord bordun on one instrument

Chord bordun on two instruments

Note that the bordun tones played by two instruments are scored to preserve the characteristic sound of the perfect fifth. Now ask the alto xylophone player to take her note for a walk. Her mallet walks to the adjacent ascending tone, returning home on every other beat. The *Boatman* score illustrates this movement of the fifth as well as the addition of two complementary color parts (the glockenspiel and the triangle).

Boatman

Trad./arr. JF

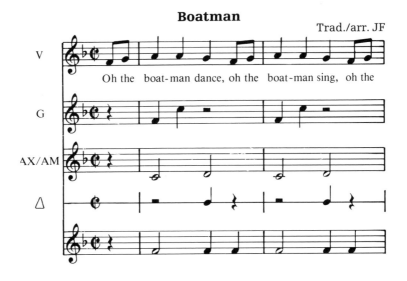

Oh the boat-man dance, oh the boat-man sing, oh the

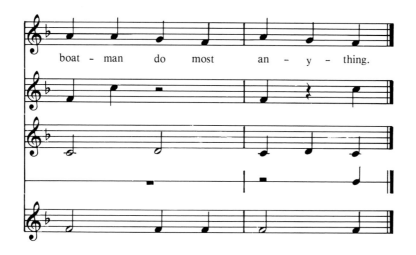

Long Legged Sailor is another illustration of the moving fifth in a different key. While rhythmic variation is achieved in the alto xylophone part, the fifth interval sounds on all strong beats. The AX moving bordun pattern may be taught by playing a regular quarter note pattern ♩ ♩ ♩ ♩ D E D E. The students may then leave out the second quarter note D (E) D E in each four-beat set.

Long Legged Sailor

Trad./arr. JF

2. short legged
3. skinny legged

4 Read, write, sing and play songs in pentatonic (F and G tonal centers)

On a Mountain is an ideal melody for notating the pentatonic scale because it contains the two motives with which the children are already familiar: *s l m* and *m r d*. The countermelody is built on the *m r d* motive in reverse. When the children have become very familiar with this countermelody they should be asked to notate it on a staff. Now ask them to write their own little pentatonic melodies based on the rhythm of the countermelody. This is a good opportunity for your students to really feel like composers and know the excitement of having classmates play their music. It is essential to play and sing *On a Mountain* in both F and G pentatonic. This will reinforce the concept of movable key centers introduced in the first grade.

On a Mountain

American/arr. JF

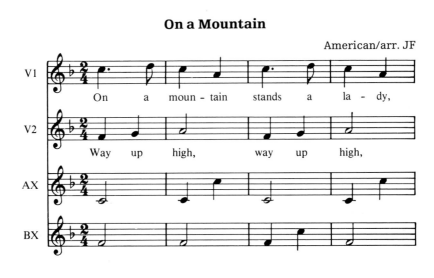

Your students can construct the melody of *Rocky Mountain* from the following motives.

Present them in scrambled fashion, then ask the children's help in organizing them in the appropriate sequence. This activity reinforces the concept of pitches moving away from and returning to the tonal center. The straightforward accompaniment could also be taught from notation. Here is the score.

Rocky Mountain

American/arr. JF

Improvisation

1 Use texts as a basis for rhythmic exploration on pitched and unpitched instruments

Texts provide an especially accessible means of using color in original ways;

this is an important step in building improvisation skills. After your children have learned a short rhyme such as

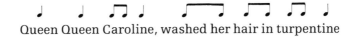

Queen Queen Caroline, washed her hair in turpentine

they can begin to use the word rhythms for unpitched color explorations. During the early stages it will help if you guide the children in suggesting such possible means of approaching this open-ended task as substituting one unpitched instrument for the text; playing the first four beats with one instrument, the second with another; and substituting unpitched instruments for certain words, e.g., 'Queen', 'hair' or rhyming words. The same idea can be applied to bar instruments. A short rhyme again provides the rhythmic material, but now the rhythm will be realized on wood and metal pitched instruments. After the children are comfortable saying and clapping the rhythm of 'Jean Jean, dressed in green, Went downtown to eat ice cream', they pat it on their thighs while you play a chord bordun on the bass xylophone.

The children now can be asked to improvise a melody based on the word rhythms of the text ($\frac{2}{4}$ ♩ ♩ | ♫ ♩ | ♫ ♫ | ♫ ♩ |). The only condition that need be imposed during these early explorations is that the melody end on *do* of the pentatonic key involved; in this case it will be G. Those using wood and metal instruments may take turns playing the first, then the second, line of the rhyme over the bass bordun. After several tries, ask the children to invent a line which they could play in the same way again. This limitation encourages students to think about the structure of their melodies. Volunteers may play their individual creations in sequence for the class. You might notate one example, demonstrating again that notation is the means by which we remember original melodies.

Another interesting possibility for pitch exploration is asking woods to improvise the entire melody while the metals play clusters of pentatonic tones only on certain text words such as 'Jean', 'green', 'eat', and the like.

Finally, all of the improvisation ideas suggested above (and they by no means exhaust the subject) can also be applied to short rhythm patterns which you provide or the class invents.

2 Build rhythmic phrases using four-beat questions and answers performed with unpitched or body percussion

Preparation for question/answer activities has taken place in the preceding step. A little chart will help children to see the framework of the eight-beat phrase which they are about to create. Ask them to clap one beat in each of the following squares.

Now they may clap in two and rest in two or clap in three and rest in one – the choice is theirs. You should then unfold the chart to its full eight-beat width and ask half of the class to clap the first four beats, half to clap the next three, resting on the last beat. Label the first four beats the question and the next four the answer. When this framework has been firmly established you may proceed through a sequence of question/answer phrase-building activities such as those outlined below.

You clap the question ♩ ♩ ♩ ♩
Children clap the answer ♩ ♩ ♩ ♩

You create a more interesting question ♩ ♩ ♫ ♩
Children try to use ♫ in their anwers (♩ ♫ ♩ ♩ is one possibility)

One child asks you a rhythmic question
You reply

You ask one child a question
Child answers

One child asks another a question
The second child answers. Reverse roles.

3 Vocally improvise a short rhyme using m r d motive

This exercise provides a reinforcement of the rhythmic and melodic motives introduced earlier. If the children have not yet discovered it, this is the time to learn that the rhythms of 'Queen Queen' and 'Jean Jean' are identical. They may choose one or the other as a text for their vocal improvisations. In my experience, the children feel most comfortable about improvising if they have first sung the entire text on each note of the *m r d* motive. (My students call these their 'Johnny-one-note' songs.) They then welcome the chance to make up their own little melodies using the now familiar three notes. A helpful atmosphere is established by sitting in a circle and moving quickly from one improvisation to another. The most effective procedure is to request the first phrase from one child, the second from the next and so on. A climate of positive support for each effort must be established at the beginning for, as we all know, children need assurance that each effort is appreciated by all.

This exercise in making something new from assimilated material is a good indicator of your children's pitch security. The class may want to remember one or two of their favorite melodies by notating them.

4 Improvise questions and answers on bar instruments using m r d motive

You have prepared your students for this activity by the bar instrument improvisation exercise and the rhythmic phrase-building sequence. One of the many possible approaches to melodic improvisation follows.

With instruments arranged in C, F or G pentatonic and using only *m r d*:

You ask a four-beat question using quarter notes; the children's answer will be three beats of quarter notes. Remind the children that the answer ends on *do* but the question does not

One child asks you a melodic question and you reply
Questions and answers again use quarter notes only

You ask one child a question and the child answers (♩ notes)

One child asks another a question; the second child answers (♩ notes)
Reverse roles

Proceed through the above steps adding eighth notes in the questions and answers

The following examples illustrate some question/answer possibilities with C, F, and G tonal centers.

Texture: Counterpoint

1 Perform speech, movement, body, and unpitched percussion ostinati as accompaniments to texts (one or two accompaniment voices)

Rhymes, poems, and sayings offer a rich variety of ostinato accompaniment possibilities. In fact, my children enjoy exploring several different media accompaniments for the same text. The *Old Witch* rhyme lends itself to a movement ostinato accompaniment which evokes the emotional quality of the text and is also well served by an unpitched percussion color accompaniment part. In the former activity, ask half of your class to take three menacing steps; the other group responds with a snatch on the fourth beat. Two groups plus a speaker may perform the piece or trios of children (one speaker, one menacing stepper, and one snatcher) present their ideas.

The unpitched accompaniment is a somewhat more straightforward procedure. It may be taught by rote or as a rhythmic reading exercise. The children will offer ideas about instrumental choices other than the guiro, or they may suggest dividing the accompaniment between two instruments. Care must be taken to maintain rhythmic accuracy during these explorations; the rhythmic tension between the spoken part and the accompaniment has to be preserved.

Old Witch

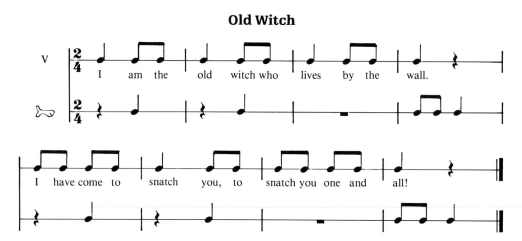

As we have seen in Chapter Two the transfer from body percussion to unpitched percussion is a very natural one. The accompaniment to the following short proverb can be prepared on the body with each child learning all of the parts. The class, divided into three groups, now plays the finger cymbal, hand drum, and hanging cymbal parts using body percussion. They continue to perform their assigned body percussion parts lightly while three children play the unpitched instruments indicated in the score. Following this extensive preparation, the three soloists should now feel comfortable about performing alone. This little sound piece, like others in this book, may be used as an introduction or interlude for a song or instrumental composition, or as an accompaniment for movement.

Ring Around the Moon

The previous activities have illustrated complementary rhythm and color contrast between the spoken text and its accompaniment. Since the accompaniment of rhymes with words does not provide color contrast, the texture must be spare to allow the principal voice part to be heard. The following example provides a bit of word play between the ostinato accompaniment and the verse.

Five Little Monkeys

2 Perform vocal ostinati as accompaniments to pentatonic melodies
This activity is suggested as the first step leading to vocal independence. Maintaining a repeated vocal part against the melody is an easier task than canon singing, though both contrapuntal experiences build musical security. Children will remember that they have already performed two melodies at the same time in *On a Mountain* (p.101). Now they will have an opportunity to sing vocal ostinati with the familiar melodies *Down the Road* and *Who's That?* (pp.107-108).

Two new melodies may now be introduced: *Great Big House* and *Jubilee* (pp.108-109). The second voice ostinato in *Jubilee* provides a good sight-singing review of *d m s* and *d r m* motives learned earlier.

Down the Road

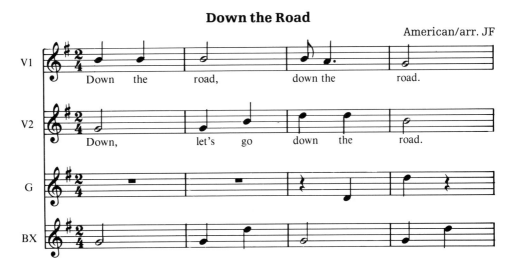

Who's That?

arr. JF

V1: Who's that tap-ping at the win-dow?

V2: Tap - ping, tap - ping, who's tap - ping?

Who's that knock-ing at the door?

Knock - ing, knock - ing, who's knock - ing?

Great Big House

arr. JF

V1: Great big house in New Or-leans, for-ty sto-reys high.

V2: Pie, pump-kin pie. Pie, pump-kin pie.

Ev - 'ry room that I've been in, filled with pump-kin pie!

Pie, pump-kin pie. Pie, pump-kin pie.

Jubilee

American/arr. JF

V1: All out on the old rail-road, all out on the sea,

V2: Look at me, I see Ju - bi - lee,

V1: All out on the old rail-road, far as I can see.

V2: Look at me, I see Ju - bi - lee.

3 Learn simple two-part rhythmic canons

The concept of overlapping imitation can be introduced through rhythmic phrases constructed from note values with which your children are by now familiar. Such material will likely be performed with contrasting body percussion colors then transferred to unpitched instruments. You might begin by writing only the first voice on the board; the children add the second voice to illustrate the texture after they have played the piece.

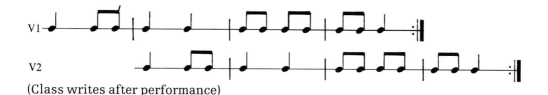

(Class writes after performance)

4 Learn simple two-part melodic canons

I've selected the following canons as first experiences because the rhythms and intervals are fairly straightforward. My students have enjoyed exchanging the cat and lady roles in *Lady Come Down*.

La - dy come down and see the cat is in the plum tree.

The lit - tle bells of West-min - ster go ding dong ding dong dong

Scot-land's burn ing, Scot-land's burn-ing. Look out, look out.

Fire, fire, fire fire, pour on wa - ter, pour on wa - ter.

* Second voice of canon enters.

Rhythm II

1 Identify ○ as ♩ ♩ ♩ ♩ and ♩ ♩

Introduction of the whole note completes the note-value vocabulary for the second-level student. Movement activities provide a means of experiencing this note in relation to those already learned. Begin by having your students walk and clap as you play the beat on the drum. At a signal have the students continue to walk the beat and clap quarters, then half, then quarters, then eighths, then quarters, and finally whole notes. At this point the class can step the various note values as you call them out or give musical cues (for example, △ = ♩). My children also enjoy playing these unpitched instrumental cues to which their classmates must respond.

110

Following this brief kinesthetic introduction to the whole note, present the symbol to the class. As we have learned in previous activities, a text offers an appropriate point of departure. The children will remember the little rhyme learned at the beginning of this level of study: 'Tic tac toe, round I go.' Now you may notate the word rhythm ♩ ♩ ♩ ♩ ♩ ♩ and ask if anyone can write it twice as fast (in diminution) ♫♩ ♫♩. Augmentation (two times slower) is, of course, the next step. You can write ♩ ♩ ? ♩ ♩ ? while children speak the text and pat the beat. How many beats on 'tic' and 'tac'? How many on 'toe'? are other kinds of questions which reinforce the concept that a whole note is four beats long (♩ ♩ ♩ ♩ = 𝅝). At this point the children can replace the question marks with 𝅝.

The class will enjoy discovering the whole note in the song *Ezekiel*.

Ezekiel Saw the Wheel

Spiritual/arr. JF

After the melody is secure, you may present a graph of the first four measures of the song which illustrates the location of the whole note. The graph is clear to children if you omit the pick-up.

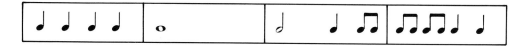

Besides isolating the whole note in a rhythmic context, this graph prepares the students for the introduction of $\frac{4}{4}$ meter in step 3 below.

2 Read, write, perform ○ and ▬ in melody and rhythm pieces
Your children should be asked to create rhythm pieces in sets of two four-beat units. One of those units must contain the whole note or its equivalent rest so that your class experiences the duration in relationship to other note values. The result might look something like this:

They should perform their own pieces, then exchange with a partner and perform the partner's piece.

Good News, (p.113), offers another example of whole notes in the song melody. These are easily detected and performed by clapping on the first beat and holding the remaining three beats. Invite your class to sing only the whole notes before singing the entire song. You may wish to graph the location of the whole notes in the melody.

If the accompaniment is added, the alto glockenspiel/soprano xylophone part can be sung with tone syllables ♩♩♩♩ ♩♩ *s s s l s m*. Next, arrange the bars in G pentatonic, then indicate the starting pitch (D) and ask the students to find the pattern based upon what they have sung.

The accompaniment of *Little Wheel* requires application of the whole-note rest. A graph helps clarify the relative amount of sound and silence in the alto xylophone part for the children.

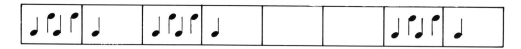

A whole-note rest should be inserted in the two empty bars. Rests can be added to fill out the three incomplete bars, as well. After the children have

Good News

Spiritual/arr. JF

Good news, Char-iots com-in', good news, Char-iots com-in', good

news, Char-iots com-in' and I don't want you to leave a me be - hind.

sung and played the entire piece they may wish to graph the soprano
xylophone part for further practice.

Little Wheel

Spiritual/arr. JF

There's a lit- tle wheel a-turn-ing in my heart, There's a

lit-tle wheel a-turn-ing in my heart, In my heart, _____ In my

heart,_____ There's a lit-tle wheel a-turn-ing in my heart.

3 Define $\frac{4}{4}$ meter. Determine bar-line placement for rhymes and rhythm patterns in $\frac{4}{4}$

Although we have been working with sets of four beats in sequence (steps 1 and 2), I have delayed a definition of meter signature in order to let experience precede theory. Once again, a text helps establish the concept.

One two three four,	Mary at the kitchen door,
Five six seven eight,	Mary at the garden gate.

Reviewing the procedure established on page 87 of this chapter we ask the children to help notate this rhyme. Adding accents helps us to group the note values into sets of four beats.

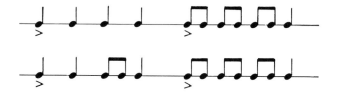

A variety of possibilities exists for exploring the new four-beat groupings. Students may walk the beat, clap the metric accents, and speak the rhyme. Or they may step the metric accents while clapping the rhyme. Or they may clap the beat, say the rhyme, and step the metric accent. The challenges are infinitely varied.

Now ask your children how they would write a four-beat meter signature. When the $\frac{4}{4}$ is agreed upon, students should be asked to think about the meter of *Ezekiel* and *Good News*. They will soon recognize that each must contain four beats because whole notes don't fit in $\frac{2}{4}$ measures. Students will want to create their own eight-beat rhythm phrases in $\frac{4}{4}$ meter for the class to perform.

4 Construct eight-beat rhythmic phrases using ♫ ♩ ♩ ᴣ ▬ ○ ▬ · Add one or two accompanying ostinato parts of varying lengths

This activity was introduced in step 2 (p.112f); now the children will extend their compositions into little pieces with added accompaniment. You might suggest working in pairs or in groups of three to construct phrases with each pair or group performing its piece for the class. Extension to sixteen beats can be created by combining two rhythmically related groups, one following the other. You can create supporting ostinato accompaniments, or two complementary phrases may be performed simultaneously.

Listening

1 Perform and listen to A B A form

The activity explored above is ideal for extending into a ternary form experience. Use percussion instruments to contrast one eight-beat phrase (A) with another (B), returning to the first again (A). Contrasting the unpitched instruments performing each section will further underline the form. A little verse may be used to illustrate this form, as well.

♩ ♩ ♩ ᴣ	
Cowboy Joe	A
♩ ♫♩ ᴣ	
From Mexico	A'
♩ ♩ ♫ ♩	
Hands up, stick 'em up	B
♩ ♩ ♩ ᴣ	
Cowboy Joe	A

Children can observe from the notation of the verse that the form is similar to that with which they have been working in their original percussion compositions. The rhythm may be transferred to bar instruments with pentatonic melodies improvised by the students.

After the students have learned the traditional cowboy song *Old Paint* by rote they will be ready to compare the form of the song to that of the rhyme.

They will discover for themselves that the first A is repeated exactly in the song, while it is varied slightly on the repetition in the poem.

Old Paint

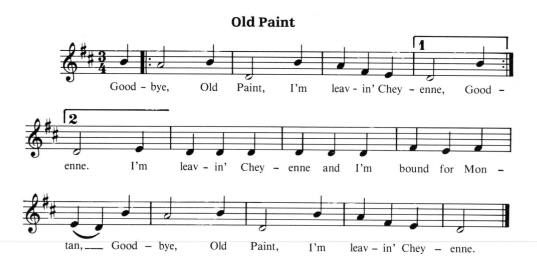

The Haydn Menuet from Divertimento in C major for piano illustrates a more elaborate version of ternary form. The A section contains within it two separate phrases based upon similar rhythmic and melodic ideas. The two repeated phrases of the B section are written in minor and major, respectively. Changes of key, as well as theme, make the return to the A section obvious to young listeners.

Menuet from Piano Sonata No. 10

Haydn

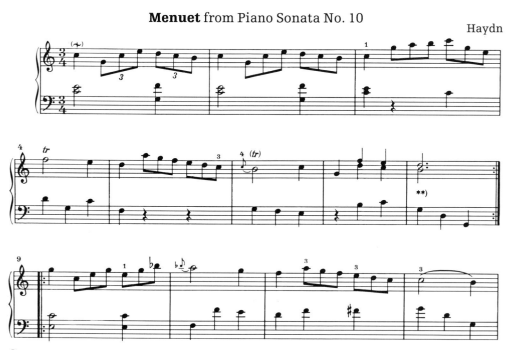

116

Trio

7 · Grade Three: Extending the Musical Vocabulary

In the first two levels of Orff instruction we placed particular emphasis on developing and using rhythmic and tonal skills. In Grade Three this material is first reviewed and then used as a foundation for a sizeable increase in vocabulary. There are eight goals.

1. To introduce students to the idea and the experience of music in triple meter. By this grade your children have had much practice with duple rhythms — they've sung, played, moved, spoken, and written them. Once secure, and by this time that should be the case, they are ready for the contrast. The dotted half note is now added to their notation vocabulary.

2. To focus on melodic notation by helping students to master the absolute pitch names of the treble clef. This is a new and crucially important vocabulary for your students to have at their disposal. I have delayed its introduction to this point so as to minimize confusion with *solfege*, the terminology they have used since the first grade. With this new knowledge, students will be able to identify by name the pentatonic key centers with which they are already familiar.

3. To expand the musical vocabulary of your class by performing contrapuntal texture in a variety of ways. At this level, children should be able to sing three-part canons, melodies with one or two vocal ostinato parts and countermelodies.

4. To use *la* as the tonal center. This is the beginning of understanding the minor scale and complements the earlier work done with *do*-centered material. One reward for your students is the sizeable amount of American folk material they can now begin to understand. The possibilities for improvisation are also enriched and children are quick to grasp them; these are new sounds which students like to make. These steps also foreshadow the introduction of the full minor scale in Grade Five.

5. To encourage improvisation, an emphasis begun in Grade One. Students use texts, rhythmic phrases and pitch to create new music; especially challenging will be the effort to improvise eight- and twelve-beat compositions.

6. To introduce new accompaniments. The first of these is a more challenging version of the simple bordun introduced in Grade Two; this material also provides a link with Grade Two and in addition prepares the class for a new accompaniment presented in Grade Four. In both cases, your students learn a greater variety of ways to use their Orff instruments.

7. To introduce *fa*. I delay it to this point in order to first assure that students can accurately sing pentatonic scale intervals. Now they should be ready for the challenge of singing and playing music that includes the half-step interval between *sol* and *mi*.

8. We conclude the year as we did Grades One and Two. Then as now the listening exercise has the dual purpose of introducing your class to music it cannot perform while providing a modest review of material covered to date. In this instance your children use their literacy skills to read sections of a rondo form.

Listed below are the goals for the year and the steps designed to achieve them.

Rhythm
1 Contrast duple with triple meter using movement
2 Define $\frac{3}{4}$ meter. Determine bar-line placement for rhymes and songs in $\frac{3}{4}$
3 Perform $\frac{3}{4}$ meter in songs and in pitched and unpitched percussion pieces. Conduct triple meter
4 Take four-measure rhythmic dictation using all note values

Melody Notation
1 Learn absolute pitch names of the treble clef
2 Identify pentatonic tonal centers of C, F, and G

Texture: Counterpoint
1 Perform speech, movement, body, or unpitched ostinati as accompaniments to texts (two complementary accompaniment parts)
2 Perform body percussion canons from imitation
3 Develop canons using movement and vocal sounds
4 Perform vocal contrapuntal material: melodies with vocal ostinati, melodies with a second complementary voice part, and three-part canons
5 Perform instrumental canons

Melody
1 Add low *la* to the tonal vocabulary
2 Identify *la* tonal center pentatonic
3 Add low *sol* to the tonal vocabulary
4 Add *fa* to the tonal vocabulary. Read, write, sing, and play in the keys of C and G

Improvisation I
1 Improvise with instruments and voices in pentatonic using texts, rhythmic phrases, and question/answer phrase building

Accompaniments
1 Perform arpeggiated bordun accompaniments for pentatonic songs and instrumental pieces
2 Perform moving bordun accompaniments to songs and instrumental pieces (one player)

Improvisation II
1 Create introductions, interludes, and codas for songs and instrumental pieces

119

Listening

1 Perform, create, and listen to rondo form

Rhythm

1 Contrast duple with triple meter using movement

As we learned in Chapter Six, a variety of movement activities is an excellent way to begin the introduction to a new meter. Our point of departure is duple; we explore triple in contrast to the material taught in Grade Two. This approach is particularly effective because the body responses of the children kinesthetically reinforce the distinction between duple and triple meter. Two of the many possible in-place movement activities to distinguish duple from triple meter include bending knees on downbeats of twos and threes (the 'kneesees' game) and arm circles in the air in front of the body (the 'ferris wheel' game). These games simulate conducting and may be combined; they are especially effective when played with recorded or improvised music.

Another meter game which my children enjoy is walking with a partner when duple is played, in trios when triple is played, and in quartets when quadruple is played on my drum. Students welcome the challenge of making up combinations of locomotor movements to illustrate meter, as well. Walk walk walk walk walk walk jump jump is an example of this in triple.

Pulses may be grouped in twos and threes by stepping the beat and clapping on the first of a set of two or a set of three. Another possibility is to step only on the first beat of a two-beat or a three-beat measure while you play rhythm patterns on a drum. When the children are comfortable stepping triple meter, they can be challenged to clap on the second or third, as well as the first, beats in the measure. Finally, children in three lines can demonstrate triple meter by clapping on assigned first, second, or third beats. After this is mastered, substitute a step for each clap. They will enjoy performing their movement activity with a musical example such as the Mozart Minuet for piano, K.94 or another short piece in triple meter.

2 Define $\frac{3}{4}$ meter. Determine bar-line placement for rhymes and songs in $\frac{3}{4}$

Following several activities of the kind suggested in the previous step, your students will be ready for the symbolic representation of triple meter. Ask them to say the rhyme:

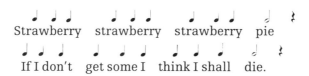

Invite the class to determine accent placement in the rhyme and then introduce bar lines as you did for duple meter in Grade Two. Other rhymes which are useful for this purpose are:

Witches ride switches across the sky. . .[1]

No one can tell us, Nobody knows,
Where the wind comes from, Where the wind goes[2]

Accent placement for songs is another useful meter exploration device. After the children have learned the song *Softly*, ask them to pat the beats while singing and invite one student to play the metric accents on finger cymbals.[3] The class will have no trouble writing the first phrase in rhythmic notation, adding bar lines in the appropriate places.

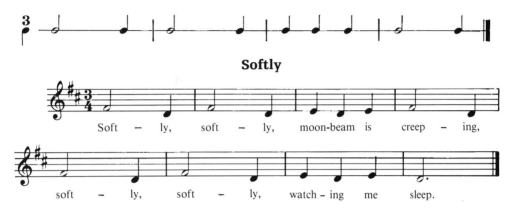

Softly

Soft — ly, soft — ly, moon-beam is creep — ing,

soft — ly, soft — ly, watch – ing me sleep.

At this point, the children ought to be ready to use their vocabulary of note values to construct a variety of three-beat measures. Here are a few examples.

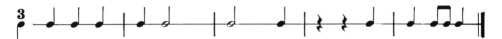

It is a good idea to review the means of filling up a $\frac{2}{4}$ and a $\frac{4}{4}$ measure with a single note (♩ and ○) before demonstrating ♩ ♩ ♩ to accomplish the same thing for a $\frac{3}{4}$ measure. Your class will realize that this can also be written ♩ ♩. A dot is now substituted for the quarter note and the class has the necessary information to write the second phrase of *Softly* in rhythmic notation.

When your students are comfortable with triple meter rhythm patterns they are ready to try inventing four-measure phrases. You might consider setting minimal requirements for these compositions such as the need to end with a dotted half-note or requiring that one of the measures contain three quarter-notes. These restrictions have the merit of better enabling you to see if your class truly understands the material. I also find it helpful to have small groups of children perform their work for the class.

3 Perform $\frac{3}{4}$ meter in songs and in pitched and unpitched percussion pieces. Conduct triple meter

The Louisana French song *Fais Dodo* contains no new melodic challenges but it offers the opportunity to explore several interesting meter activities. The notes might first be placed on the board with no metric indication ♪♪♪♪♪♪♪ *m r d d r d r m*. The children will readily agree to try something more interesting, such as adding bar lines after every two notes. The appropriate meter signature is now added ($\frac{2}{4}$) and a slight stress is given to the first beat of each measure while singing. But the results remain musically unsatisfying. You might now suggest yet another alteration, changing the first note of each group to a half note ♩ ♩ ♩ ♩ ♩ ♩ ♩ ♩ which the class will agree sounds 'right'. They will realize that the meter signature must also be changed to accommodate the new rhythmic content of the measures. A comparison of the actual score of the song to this solution reveals a difference only in the third measure. After my children learn the text of the lullaby they find singing it in duple meter greatly amusing. Concept learning through this kind of experiment and comparison is very interesting to students because it involves them in the learning process in an active way.

Fais Dodo

Louisiana French/arr. JF

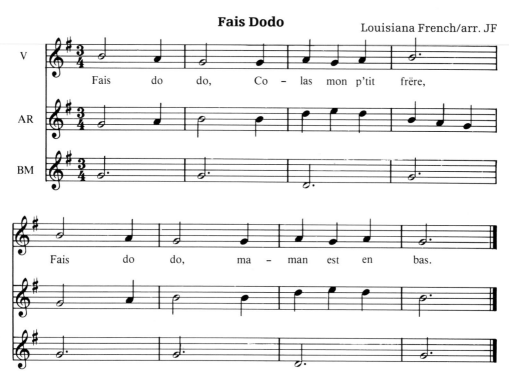

Fais do do, Co - las mon p'tit frère,

Fais do do, ma - man est en bas.

Unpitched instrumental pieces, typically prepared through body percussion activities, are an important means of building performance security in all meters. We begin with a simple rhythmic exercise which is related to the melodic rhythm of *Fais Dodo*.[4]

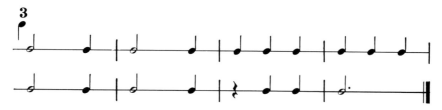

122

You may ask the children to clap quarter notes and pat the half and dotted half, to clap the metric accents and pat beats two and three, or to substitute unpitched instruments for the various note values. A complementary ostinato in a different body or unpitched percussion color may be added to the rhythm, such as:

The opportunity for improvisation should not be overlooked. Ask the students to think the rhythm of the first six measures, clapping only the last two. Now they may improvise their own rhythm patterns in triple meter for the first six measures, but they must play seven and eight as written. Meter and phrase length are given; tone color and most of the rhythmic content are chosen by the students.

The following more elaborate example is scored for three parts; children should be encouraged to create their own two-voice compositions based on this model. Four-measure phrase lengths and complementary rhythms are two important composition devices to keep in mind when constructing rhythm pieces.

Pitched instrument pieces are another means of reinforcing skill in performance of triple meters. The next composition is appropriate for players at this level; note the relationship of the melodic rhythm to the rhythmic exercise introduced on p.122.[5] Student conductors should be selected after the class has practiced the triple meter conducting pattern.

Improvisations based on this piece may be developed by analyzing the syllable names of the pitches used and identifying the repeated measures based on the ♩ ♩ rhythm. Ask your students to use the same rhythmic content and repeated motive but a new arrangement of pitches in their improvisations.

4 Take four-measure rhythmic dictation using all note values

You will remember that the 'Big Ears Game' was introduced in Grade Two to evaluate student progress in rhythm mastery. We continue that idea at this level, now substituting four-*measure* for four-*beat* units. In this new challenge students are asked to write note values in a variety of meters from your clapped patterns. Here are four examples appropriate to use at this point in the sequence. You may develop more challenging exercises as the children's rhythmic abilities grow.

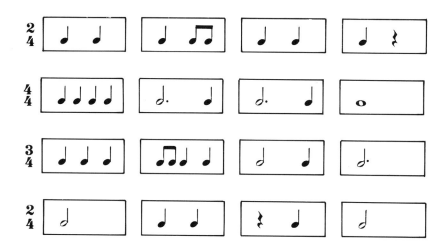

Melodic Notation

1 Learn absolute pitch names of the treble clef

During the second level of instruction we asked the children to master only one system of naming pitches: tone syllables. The new tonal nomenclature they will be taught in this level is absolute pitch names. Fortunately, Orff students are already familiar with them since their instrument bars are identified by pitch names (C, D, etc).

A 'handy' aid to learning names of the lines and spaces is the hand staff, which children first encounter on a worksheet. This diagram clarifies the relationship of the five fingers to the five lines.

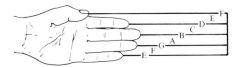

After the children have labelled the lines and spaces appropriately they should make an authentic hand staff by holding one hand across the front of the body, palm facing inward. The index finger of the other hand is used to point to the 'lines and spaces' of the hand staff. The middle C ledger line is created by placing the thumb of the pointing hand under the little finger (E) of the hand staff. Children can practice with partners or in teams until everyone has mastered the absolute pitch names of the treble clef.

The *Note Name Duet* provides practice in reading names of lines and spaces. The piece may be performed on bar instruments when the children can sing the letter names of all parts with rhythmic accuracy.

Note Name Duet

JF

Where is John is a more challenging piece for note-name practice. It may be sung in unison or in a two- or three-part canon before transfer to the instruments takes place. I've added a simple ostinato to practice the note names below the tonal center. Since the purpose of this piece is drill on lines and spaces, the text should be added last, if at all.

Where is John?
The old black hen has left her pen! Oh!
Where is John?
The cows are in the corn again.
Oh John! Oh John! Oh Johnny!

Where is John?

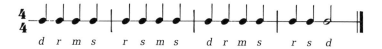

2 Identify pentatonic tonal centers of C, F, and G

You will remember that we worked with pentatonic tonal centers in Grade
Two by establishing various *do* locations. Since absolute pitch names are now
familiar to the children, they will identify the C, F, and G pentatonic centers
by name. This step is made readily comprehensible to the class by the visual
reinforcement of the pitch-labelled bar instruments.

To begin, ask the children to arrange their instruments in C pentatonic (F
and B bars removed) and to sing *Aunt Dinah* with syllables.

When they have memorized it, ask them to find their tune on the bar
instruments in C-*do*. Now ask them to play a chord bordun (C and G) while
they sing the melody with syllables. If you start the singers on F the point will
be quickly made that melody and accompaniment must agree on *do*.

Instruments now play the melody transposed to F and G tonal centers, with
appropriate borduns added on dulcimer, guitar, or bass. Assign specific tonal
centers to various instrumental voices: for example, glockenspiels play C,
soprano xylophones and metallophones play F, and alto instruments play G;
then compare the results. For·a further challenge, think the first and third
measures but play the second and fourth in all three tonal centers. You can
encourage melodic exploration by asking the students to (1) choose a tonal

center, then (2) sing the first and third measures with a new order of pitches and (3) play the second and fourth measures as written.

Finally, writing *Aunt Dinah* on the staff gives the children further practice in understanding tonal centers. C, F, or G may serve as *do*; most of your children will find that they can now write the melody from memory.

Aunt Dinah (In three moods)

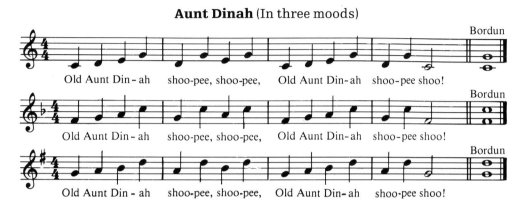

Texture: Counterpoint

1 Perform speech, movement, body, or unpitched ostinati as accompaniments to texts (two complementary accompaniment parts)
Speech and body percussion accompaniments add textural interest to rhymes, verses, and poems. That interest is enhanced by color contrast between the parts. Speech accompaniments must be especially spare to avoid covering the verse. The interesting effect obtained by adding vocables to a text setting can be observed in the following score.

Johnny

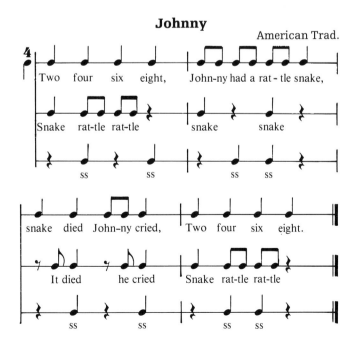

127

The next score illustrates a rhyme accompanied by body percussion. This piece requires two accompaniment groups performing complementary rhythms to one another and to the text. The children's musicianship is stretched when they are asked to perform the voice and one of the two accompaniment parts simultaneously.

Papa Moses

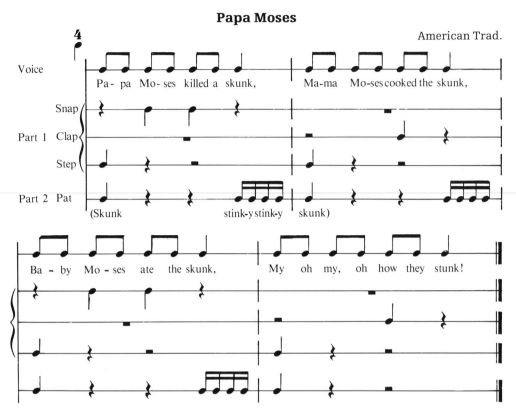

American Trad.

Movement accompaniment evokes the nuances of a rhyme or poem in an especially distinctive way. In this medium particularly, children will contribute a variety of ideas which makes the experience uniquely their own. Suggestions which avoid a literal depiction of the text should be encouraged, though poems such as the following contain compelling realistic imagery.

Praise Song of the Wind
Trees with weak roots
I will strike, I the wind
I will roar, I will whistle

Houses not tightly roofed
I will destroy, I the wind
I will roar, I will whistle

Hay piled in sheds
I will tear apart, I the wind
I will roar, I will whistle

Traditional Siberian

2 Perform body percussion canons from imitation

Children were introduced to the concept of overlapping imitation in Grade Two. Now they are ready to apply the principle to a canon performed in spontaneous imitation of your body percussion sounds.

Echo clapping four-beat patterns is a typical means of preparing this exercise. First, develop the canon by beginning a four-beat pattern which the class imitates at the interval of one measure while you continue with a new pattern on a different body percussion color. It is likely that the class will succeed if you alternate difficult with easier patterns and avoid mixing body percussion colors within the measure. The following score illustrates a two-part percussion canon.

A three-part canon provides a real concentration challenge for you and the class. In this exercise one group of students follows you, a second group follows the first. The leader must be careful to maintain contrast in both rhythmic content and body color.

3 Develop canons using movement and vocal sounds

A variety of media offers children new opportunities for enriching their understanding of overlapping imitation. For instance, movement canons provide a visual and kinesthetic reinforcement of the concept. Without music, begin by exploring such nonlocomotor movements as bending, stretching, swinging, twisting, shaking, pushing, pulling, and bouncing. Develop a sequence of four, perhaps accompanied by appropriate percussion instruments. Instrument cues or a predetermined series of beats (five or six, for example) can determine the duration of each movement. Then, divide the class into three groups and have them perform the movement sequence in a two-part canon while one group watches. The audience group not only observes the contrapuntal texture but also stimulates a careful performance. The possibilities for contrasting locomotor movements, movement qualities, levels, direction, and tempo are limitless. Bar and percussion instrument contrapuntal compositions and art music can also serve to stimulate movement ideas.

Canons may also be developed with vocables. A series of several varying vocal colors can provide interesting material for contrapuntal treatment as illustrated in the following four-part canon.

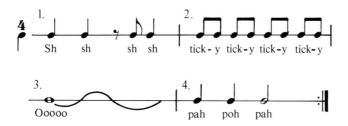

Your class may wish to combine the two activities presented above. Vocables may be added to express qualities of, or serve as the inspiration for, movement canons.

4 Perform vocal contrapuntal material: melodies with vocal ostinati, melodies with a second complementary voice part, and three-part canons

As we have seen in Grade Two, the addition of a vocal ostinato to the melody facilitates vocal independence. *I Want to Rise* and *Fisherman Peter* (p.131) present two examples of vocal ostinati suitable for Grade Three students.

A second complementary voice part, unlike the vocal ostinato, is not constructed from repeated patterns and may, therefore, prove to be somewhat

I want to Rise

American/arr. JF

I want to rise in the ear - ly morn,

Ear - ly, I think it's much too

I want to rise in the ear - ly morn, I want to rise in the

ear - ly, I think it's much too ear - ly,

ear - ly morn, and I'll nev-er sleep late a-ny more.

I think it's much too ear - ly, I think I'll sleep.

Fisherman Peter

Spiritual/arr. JF

Fish-er-man Pe - ter on the sea, Drop your

Pe - ter, fish-er-man Pe - ter, fol-low, fol-low me,

net boy and fol - low me.

Pe - ter, fish-er-man Pe - ter, fol - low, fol - low me.

more difficult to master. In the following example both voice parts begin on the same note in each phrase but the last, as an aid to young singers.

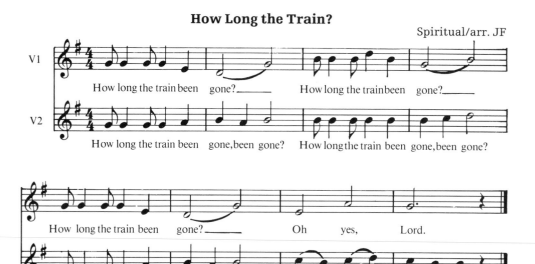

How Long the Train?

Spiritual/arr. JF

The devices of vocal ostinato and complementary voice part have been combined in the following three-part piece. After the children have learned the melody you may add the third voice ostinato. When these parts are secure, voice two may be sung at sight from notation and added to the ensemble.

Noah's Ark

American/arr. JF

Canons are the most typical examples of vocal polyphonic material. The following have been selected for their accessibility of range and comfortable intervals. Further, they present an opportunity for reinforcement of Grade Three skills and concepts: $\frac{3}{4}$ meter and/or hexatonic melody (the addition of the fourth scale degree to be presented in the next section of this sequence).

La Cloche

Din   don   din   don,   c'est   la   clo-che   du   ma-tin.

Qui sonne au   le   –   ver   du   jour :   bon   –   jour,   bon   –   jour!

Morning is Come

Morn – ing   is   come,   night   is   a – way.

Rise   with   the   sun_____   and __   wel – come   the   day.

Lovely Evening

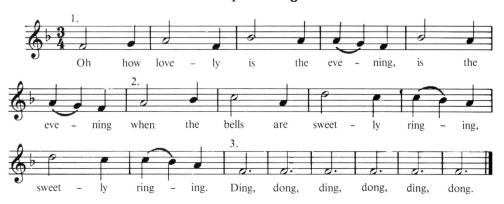

Oh   how   love – ly   is   the   eve – ning,   is   the

eve – ning   when   the   bells   are   sweet – ly   ring – ing,

sweet – ly   ring – ing. Ding,   dong,   ding,   dong,   ding,   dong.

5 *Perform instrumental canons*

133

The above rhythm canons may be prepared through body percussion and transferred to unpitched instruments.[6] The results are most effective when two different instruments are used to make the timbre contrasts clear.

The melodic canon exercises below may be performed on bar instruments or recorder.[7] Children also enjoy transferring vocal canons to the instruments.

Melody

1 Add low la to the tonal vocabulary

Adding low *la* to your students' pentatonic vocabulary offers new intervals for sight singing and prepares them for the introduction of *la*-centered pentatonic. The following melody provides a point of departure.

Who Built the Ark?

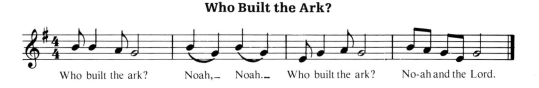

Who built the ark?   Noah,— Noah.—   Who built the ark?   No-ah and the Lord.

After the children are familiar with the melody of *Who Built the Ark?*, ask them to read the notation of the last measure from score.

They will observe that one of the notes sounds different from the tune they know. Now help them identify the note and substitute low *la* for the tone in question.

134

With this tonal information the children can sing the countermelody to *Who Built?* at sight.

No - ah built the ark, No - ah built the ark.

Train's Off the Track is not an easy melody for children to sing at first sight. However, if you provide isolated motives, the class will gain accessibility to the melody as a whole. Using this approach the children read:

Students now listen for the appearance of these motives as you sing the song. They then may sing motives one, two, and three when they occur at the appropriate place in the song. After your children feel secure with the tonal material, they may be introduced to the score of the entire melody. Accompaniment may be provided by a broken bordun.

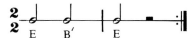

This song introduces *la* tonal center.

Train's off the Track

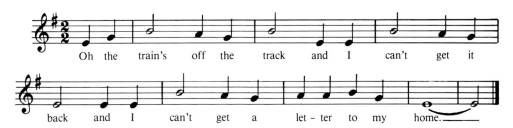

Oh the train's off the track and I can't get it
back and I can't get a let - ter to my home.

2 Identify la *tonal center pentatonic*

Before they see the score of *Chicka Hanka* have your students name the following notes.

You might then point out that this is a G pentatonic scale with *sol* and *la* at the beginning, instead of the end, of the scale. Another way to look at this arrangement is:

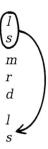

Students are now ready to see the *Chicka Hanka* melody. After the first and last notes have been identified, they will realize that the notes belong to the G pentatonic scale, but the tonal center is *la*. Then explain to the class that the bordun must also be built on *la* and ask the students to discover the bordun tones, E and B. After the glockenspiel part is prepared vocally (♩ ♩ ♩ | ♩ ♩) it may be transferred to the instrument and added to the BX accompaniment. The AX part needs considerable rhythmic preparation and should be added last.

Chicka Hanka

American/arr. JF

Cap-tain   go   side – track your   train. _____

Num-ber three in   line,   Com- in' in   on   time.

3 Add low sol to the tonal vocabulary

Your class has already met low *sol* in the previous step; now we emphasize it
it a new song. But first, take time to review the scale arrangement just
presented.

You might isolate the first four notes of this scale and ask the group to listen
for this motive as you sing *Miss Susan Brown*. Then ask the children to play
measure one backwards on a bar instrument; this illustrates the motive in
reverse in the second phrase of the song. Low *sol* and *la* can also be found in
the AX accompaniment part. It is a good idea to sing this ostinato before
playing it.

Miss Susan Brown

American/arr. JF

Hold my mule while I dance, Jo-sie, Hold my mule while I dance, Jo-sie,

Hold my mule while I dance, Jo-sie, Hel-lo Su-san Brown.

Low *sol* and *la* are used in the accompaniment of *Oh, Won't You Sit Down?* Your children will very likely recognize this as another rhythmic variation of the moving bordun they learned in Grade Two and performed in *Miss Susan Brown*. Someone with attentive ears is certain to point out the low *sol la sol* motive in the song melody.

Oh, Won't You Sit Down?

Spiritual/arr. JF

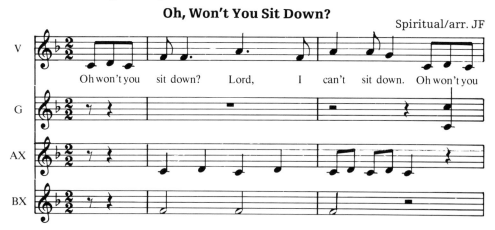

Oh won't you sit down? Lord, I can't sit down. Oh won't you

138

For further practice ask the children to write low *sol* and *la* from G *do* on a staff. Now ask them to write three motives: $s_1 \, l_1 \, d$, *m m r r d* and *m m m d*.

Now sing *Shake Those 'Simmons Down* on loo and ask the children to check their motive sheets to discover the number of times they hear each motive. They may want to arrange their motives in the order in which they appear in the song.

Shake Those 'Simmons Down

4 Add fa *to the tonal vocabulary. Read, write, sing and play in the keys of C and G*

As we have seen many times in this book, children are led to the unfamiliar from the familiar. This procedure is encountered again in the following lesson; a known melodic cell paves the way for the introduction of the new note, *fa*.

After the children have sung this cell at sight, present them with the motive written in sequence a third higher.

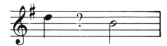

The note in question is introduced as *fa*. Now give them the score of *Chairs to Mend* which they have first learned to sing by rote. After all of the *fa* tones are located, have the class sing the canon with syllables, adding the BX on half notes to secure the tempo. The moving fifth will be read from score and added to the ensemble later.

Chairs to Mend

Trad./arr. JF

Ask your students to review the familiar canon *La Cloche*. Now that they have added *fa* to their tonal repertoire they should be able to write measures three and four in the key of C. They will recognize the sequence when they attempt the next two measures.

Transfer to the instruments is optional. If your children wish to play the canon, the note writing, syllable singing, and note name identification will have prepared them for instrumental performance.

The glockenspiel part in *Frog in a Bog* provides an opportunity to practice sight-singing a melody which includes *fa* and which contains no rhythmic difficulties. Patience at this point is particularly important; singing intervals accurately is difficult for many children and is most successfully accomplished when taken slowly.

Frog in a Bog

American/arr. JF

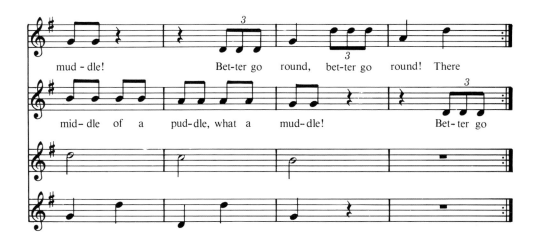

mud - dle! Bet-ter go round, bet-ter go round! There

mid- dle of a pud-dle, what a mud-dle! Bet-ter go

Improvisation I

1 Improvise with instruments and voices in pentatonic using texts, rhythmic phrases, and question/answer phrase building

Vocal improvisation

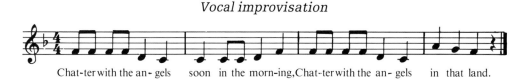

Chat-ter with the an- gels soon in the morn-ing, Chat-ter with the an- gels in that land.

After the children have read *Chatter With the Angels* at sight, you should ask them to sing the tone cells of the melody.

Each child should try to sing four beats of 'angel chatter' (angels presumably sing tone syllables) based on either of the two tone cells. Rhythms should be very simple at first (♩ ♩) to permit concentration on the tones in question. Eighth notes may be added when the tones are secure and students are ready for a greater challenge.

When your class is comfortable singing their made-up melodies a little form may be created. Have three children sing four beats based on the first cell in

142

succession with all children singing *mi re do* on the fourth measure. One example of a result might be:

Instrumental, using text. We have seen that words provide a convenient rhythmic structure for pentatonic instrumental improvisation in Grade Two. This level introduces the same idea but now prescribes both *do* and *la*-centered pentatonic improvisation. Children are fascinated to hear the transformation which occurs in a given rhythm when its tonal center shifts from *do* to *la*. Although composition is not the goal here, students may want to notate some of their favorite *Tweedle Dee* instrumental creations.[8]

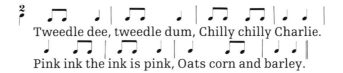

Tweedle dee, tweedle dum, Chilly chilly Charlie.

Pink ink the ink is pink, Oats corn and barley.

Rhythmic phrases. Your students encountered an example of a piece for bar instruments developed from a rhythmic exercise on pages 122ff. Now they will improvise their own melodies based on given rhythmic phrases. Invite the class to decide what pentatonic scale to use and whether to work with *do* or *la* center. In preparation for playing on instruments, the rhythmic phrase should be spoken with rhythm syllables, clapped, patted on thighs, and finally played on the tonal center. Add a second and third note on each repetition of the phrase until all five tones are being used. As usual in these improvisation exercises, it makes sense to establish one or two guidelines for your students. You might ask that they begin and end on the tonal center and that they repeat the same pitches for two motives. These simple rules will help you to determine how well the class is in control of the material. Here are some phrases to use as a basis for improvisation on bar instruments.

Question/answer phrase building on instruments. The question/answer device used to create musical phrases is a familiar idea to children. Pitch material for improvisation is extended from three tones to five in Grade Three; a dulcimer or guitar often provides the bordun foundation for melodic improvisations. The outline presented in Grade Two (pp.104-105) may offer some points of departure; however, most children will now enjoy working in a framework of eight-beat questions and answers of the same length. In order to assure that attention is focused on the contributions of each pair of improvisers, you might occasionally ask the class to echo sing a particular question or answer. Improvisations can serve as introductions to or contrasting sections for songs and instrumental pieces.

In no other activity is development of musical skill as obvious as in improvisation activities. Vocal and mallet technique, rhythmic competence, and melodic security are all clearly demonstrated when a student is improvising.

Accompaniments

1 Perform arpeggiated bordun accompaniments for pentatonic songs and instrumental pieces

The arpeggiated bordun style is the last to be introduced because it is the most technically challenging. I find it best to prepare the class by reviewing the simple bordun — patting left hand on left thigh, right hand on right thigh. Now the children leave their right hands on right thighs while the left joins the right hand on the right thigh. After every child has accomplished this task, ask the class to play left hand on left thigh and right hand on right thigh followed by both hands on right thigh on every other beat. Only after this is secure should you proceed to alternating the hands from the broken bordun to crossing the left *over* the right hand, the last step in the body preparation. The diagram illustrates the progression from broken to arpeggiated bordun.

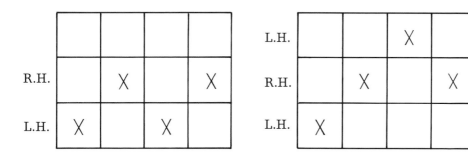

Broken bordun   Arpeggiated bordun

The arpeggiated bordun is introduced in the AX part in *Redbird*. All the children will want to try out on an instrument what they have practiced on their bodies; you might give every child a turn to try both quarter- and eighth-note crossing patterns before the full orchestration is developed.

Here Stands a Redbird

American/arr. JF

2 Perform moving bordun accompaniments to songs and instrumental pieces (one player)

The accompaniment for *Chairs to Mend* performed earlier on alto and bass xylophone may now be performed by one player on the bass. The AX player demonstrates her part by using two hands, then repeats it using her right hand alone. She adds the tonic in her left hand and performs both parts simultaneously on the bass. All of the children should have an opportunity to try this part.

Oh Watch the Stars offers another opportunity to perform a moving bordun in the bass.[9] The two examples illustrate the decoration of the fifth scored below the voice parts for support.

Oh Watch the Stars

American/arr. JF

Improvisation II

1 Create introductions, interludes, and codas for songs and instrumental pieces

I suggested earlier in this chapter (pp.143-144) that phrase-building improvisations be incorporated into the children's songs and instrumental pieces. It should be interesting for the children to review some of their favorite material from the year, now adding an original introduction, interlude or coda. Beginning efforts include unpitched percussion instruments for special effects such as guiro, cabasa, and train whistle for *Chicka Hanka*. I let the children determine the organization of these sounds.

Voices and instruments will also be used to extend songs and instrumental pieces. While texts suggest the kind of sound effect or melodic style most appropriate for the vocal material, bar instrument pieces might benefit from the contrast of an unpitched beginning, middle, or final section.

Listening

Perform, create, and listen to rondo form

The rondo (or French *rondeau*) offers children an opportunity to extend their understanding of sectional form. The idea of a given theme contrasted with a second was introduced in Grade One; two contrasting themes with a return to the first was encountered in Grade Two. Now they are asked to listen for the return of a given theme following the presentation of at least two contrasting melodies. Your students will be prepared for this assignment by first participating in a rondo performance.

The following melodic rondo is only one of several suggestions for making rondos to be found in *Music for Children*, American Edition, Vol. II, pp. 39-41.

Ex. 3. Instrumental rondo in contrasting moods

After the children have successfully completed this exercise, play Rondoapplause (Klatschrondo) from the recording *Streetsong* [(HC25122) BASF, 1975]. They invariably want to create their own 'applause' rondos based on this model. Finally, their ears will be ready for an example from the art music literature written by Rameau. This piece is well received by children because they can easily follow the form and they are fascinated by the sound of the harpiscord.[10] You should play the A theme several times, asking the class to first clap the rhythm lightly, then sing the theme along with you.

La Villageoise

Rameau

A surprise awaits them when the recording is played: the theme is not performed in this straightforward way, but rather, is elaborately embellished. The children will recognize that the excitement of the contrasting C section is created by faster rhythm; these sixteenth-note figures are retained in the final return to A.

La Villageoise (The Village Maid)

Rondeau

Rameau

8 · Grade Four: Developing Musical Proficiency

By this time most of your students have a good comprehension of meters, pentatonic intervals, and elementary rhythms. This is excellent preparation for the rhythmic, melodic, and analytic challenges your class meets in Grade Four.

1. Our first objective is to address a variety of rhythmic problems. We begin with double division of the beat. Then the class is introduced to the eighth rest, dotted notes, and syncopation. After learning that eighth notes can be separated, students are ready for new rhythmic challenges such as ♩. ♪ , ♪♩. , ⸌ and ♪♩ ♪ . As usual, time is provided for evaluation and improvisation exercises. Finally, we focus on up-beats. Now your class not only learns the meaning of that concept but also reads it from notation, conducts, and improvises with it.

2. Our second purpose is a melodic one: to complete the tonal inventory of the diatonic scale. We begin by introducing the flatted fourth scale degree (*fa*) in the key of F. Following the introduction of *ti* students discover the arrangement of whole and half steps through singing and playing diatonic melodies in the keys of C, F, and G.

3. The class continues its exploration of texture beginning with canon singing and playing, then with two-chord accompaniments. Up to this point most melodies were accompanied by some version of the simple bordun; now the students explore melodies with harmonic implications that require a dominant chord in the accompaniment.

4. We aim in this grade as in every other to foster improvisation. As you know, not only are these exercises enjoyable challenges for your students but they are also excellent ways for you to evaluate the degree to which your class has grasped the concepts you've been teaching them. In this grade I've followed the usual pattern of sprinkling improvisation opportunities throughout the work. I've also placed near the close of the year a step which will give the class a chance to work with all of the material covered to date.

5. We conclude Grade Four with a listening exercise. As always these experiences grow out of the music studied during the year. In this instance Purcell's Canon provides an illustration of the diatonic scale and counterpoint. Of course, no one brief composition can do justice to all the work you've done with your students. You will surely wish to add other listening exercises that do what this Canon does not.

Listed below are the goals for the year and the steps designed to accomplish them.

Rhythm
1 Read, write, sing, and play ♩♪♪♪♩

2 Introduce division of the beat into ♪♬ and ♬♪; read, write, sing and play
3 Read, write, and perform 𝄾 in songs and instrumental pieces
4 Perform syncopated rhythm pattern ♪♩ ♪
5 Read, write, sing, and play dotted quarter-note rhythm patterns and ♩. ♪, ♪♩.
6 Take rhythmic dictation: eight- and twelve-beat patterns using all learned note values
7 Read, write, sing, and play pieces beginning with up-beats. Conduct up-beats

Melody
1 Add *fa* in the key of F. Recognize the need for the flatted fourth scale degree
2 Add *ti* to the tonal vocabulary in C and F
3 Recognize the need for the raised seventh scale degree (*ti*) in the key of G
4 Write key signatures in C, F, and G diatonic

Texture
1 Sing three- and four-part diatonic canons
2 Sing chord roots and play pieces requiring a I-V harmonic setting on bar instruments

Improvisation
1 Create instrumental introductions, codas, and contrasting sections for song material

Listening
1 Perform and listen to examples of chaconne

Rhythm

1 Read, write, sing, and play ♬♬

Your children began to study rhythm in Grade One when they experimented with the beat and its division. In Grade Two they mastered extension of the beat to half- and whole-note durations. New rhythm skills for the third grade included learning the dotted half and $\frac{3}{4}$ meter signature. Now we begin the next step: dividing the quarter note into four parts. Children have encountered this pattern in songs and rhymes earlier in their music experiences; now we demonstrate it through sound and symbol. You will find that words and visual aids are helpful means of establishing this concept. For example, ask the children to say 'hum' in repeated quarter notes. Part of the class continues this while another section adds a new word on the after-beat, 'dum'. Accuracy is assured when the children understand that both groups say the word 'hum' together. Ask the students to notate what they have performed thus far.

hum

hum dum

After this review of the beat and its division, a new group of children says *Humpty Dumpty* while the other groups continue their 'hums' and 'dums' as performed earlier. Again, the children must be reminded that all 'hums' are spoken simultaneously. The symbols for the new words may now be introduced.

hum

hum dum

Humpty Dumpty

The concept of division and subdivision of the beat can be reinforced in a visual way other than by notation. One especially enjoyed by my children is a review of the game in which they are asked to occupy chairs representing the quarter-note beat. You will remember that a row of four chairs provided the opportunity for the children themselves to symbolize the note values ♩ and ♫. Now the class claps the various patterns created by the children after those representing sixteenth notes discover a way for *four* people to occupy *one* chair!

Rectangle graphs are also useful visual aids for representing note values. Three separate cards may be held by a line of individual children and clapped by the class.

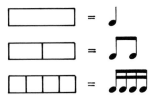

Several four-beat motives may be created by changing the cards in the sequence and adding a rest at the end.

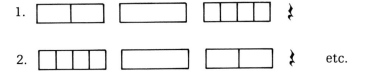

Students are eager to notate their own four-beat motives in conventional notation which include a set of four sixteenth notes on the first, second or third beat. They may wish to connect two of their motives to create an eight-beat phrase. Small groups of children should perform their compositions for one another.

The class will now be ready to sightread rhythmic phrases which include the four sixteenth notes. Two rhythmic phrases may be performed simultaneously, first on contrasting body sounds, then on unpitched percussion instruments.

Song material containing sixteenth notes provides yet another means of developing confidence in performing these new note values. Both voice parts of *Brass Wagon* contain sixteenth notes and the *Dance Josey* melody offers ♫♫♪♩on a single pitch in three of its eight measures; this rhythmic figure is echoed in the AX part.

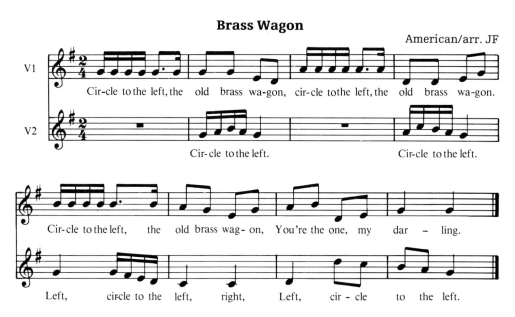

Brass Wagon

American/arr. JF

A *Brass Wagon* dance may be performed by two concentric circles facing one another; students enjoy seeing the faces of their friends as they move in opposite directions. We clap hands with a partner in the opposite circle in the last phrase and we usually change the text.

The second verse is, of course, circle to the right; on a third verse ('swing, oh swing') we perform a two-hand swing with a partner from the opposite circle.

Movement activities provide further aural awareness of the ♫♫♫ figure. You might ask your students to step quarter notes in place until they hear you play ♫♫♫ on a drum. The class walks in space only as long as they hear the

154

Dance Josey

American/arr. JF

V: Chick-en on the fence post, can't dance Jo - sey, Chick-en on the fence post, can't dance Jo - sey,

Chick-en on the fence post, can't dance Jo - sey, Hel – lo Su – san Brown!

sixteenth-note figure. A more challenging version of this idea is to ask the class to walk quarter notes. They are to stop walking when they hear ♪♬ and not resume until the figure is played again.

2 Introduce division of the beat into ♪♬ and ♬♪ ; read, write, sing, and play

Your students are now ready to practice more challenging configurations of eighth and sixteenth notes. A useful point of departure is the graph device introduced earlier. You will remember that these rectangular charts provide a visual reinforcement of note value relationships.

It is important that these charts, each of which represents only a single beat, be performed in the context of four-, six-, or eight-beat groupings since isolated charts do not provide a sense of rhythmic flow. When your students can perform a variety of note-value arrangements with confidence, they are ready for new variations on the division of the beat. They may work out the way to play ☐☐☐☐ and ☐☐☐☐ for themselves.

The relationship of these graphs to actual rhythmic notation must be made clear at the beginning. Students should then move quickly from playing a series of note values from charts to performance from notation.

Again, there is nothing like a game to help matters along. My classes like rhythmic 'tic-tac-toe' since it provides an enjoyable – and effective – way to practice a variety of note values. Begin by dividing the class into several small groups and asking each to decide on its own way of clapping three beats. They may move horizontally, vertically, or diagonally in any direction. The children not playing must guess the performance plan.

Rhythmic Tic Tac Toe

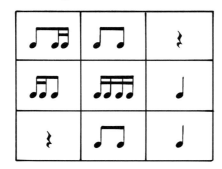

Further practice in performing eighth and sixteenth note combinations is provided through speech activities. Ask your children to find ♪♫ as they first say, then clap:

2/4 ♫ ♪♫ | ♫ ♪♫ | ♫ ♫ | ♩ ♪ ‖
How much wood could a wood chuck chuck if a wood chuck could chuck wood?

This text provides an opportunity to play a word game which is great fun. Students perform the text silently, except for the word 'wood'. Another time try only 'chuck'. Later try two groups, one assigned to each word. Finally, add a speech ostinato.

2/4 ♫♪ ♩ | ♫♪ ♩ | ♫♪ ♫♪ |
Chucky chuck wood, Chucky chuck wood, Chucky chuck, Chucky chuck

♫♪ ♩ :‖
Chucky chuck wood.

156

Isolating the eighth- and sixteenth-note combinations in songs is another way to practice the rhythmic figures. *Toembai* is a good choice for both ♪♫ and ♬. After the children can perform it as a three-part canon, they should try it on three groups of contrasting unpitched percussion colors.

Toembai

Israeli

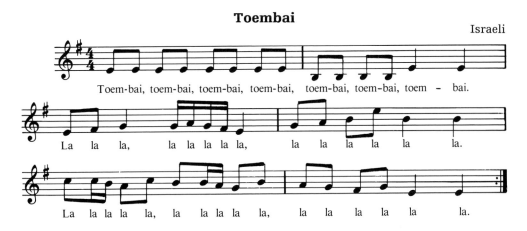

Toem-bai, toem-bai, toem-bai, toem-bai, toem-bai, toem-bai, toem - bai.

La   la   la,   la la la la la,   la   la   la   la   la   la.

La   la la la   la,   la   la la la   la,   la   la   la   la   la   la.

Draw a Bucket contains both ♬ and ♪♫ figures. They can be practiced by dividing the class into two groups, each responsible for clapping one phrase of the second section of the song.

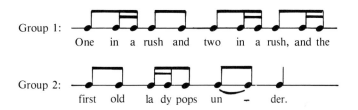

Group 1:

One in a rush and two in a rush, and the

Group 2:

first   old   la dy pops un - der.

Draw a Bucket of Water

American/arr. JF

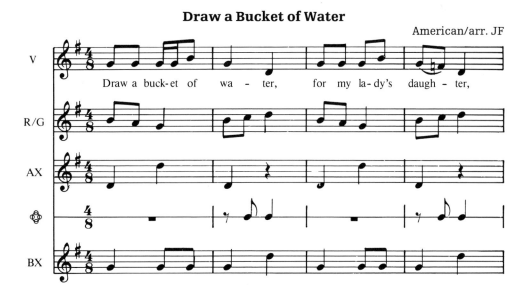

Draw a buck-et of   wa - ter,   for my la-dy's   daugh - ter,

Improvisation using the new sixteenth-note figures can be initiated by isolating motives from a new melody.

Vol. III, p. 111

After you have sung this on loo or played it on your recorder, ask the children to arrange the rhythmic motives from notation in the order that they appear in the following song.

Dundai

Israeli

Count the number of beats in each pattern, add four more at the end of each, and clap each eight-beat phrase. Four groups of students, each assigned a pattern, may develop new eight-beat phrases; the only limitation is that the given four-beat pattern must be present in the phrase. Interest is heightened if you keep the assignments a secret; the class must guess which pattern the performing group was assigned. Students should now be prepared to do the same assignment individually; move around the class several times to allow children second chances to correct mistakes or, if successful the first time, to try a new motive.

3 Read, write, perform ⁷ in songs and instrumental pieces

Students have been working with eighth notes in pairs to this point. Now, in preparation for the eighth rest, syncopated, and dotted figures to follow, you should separate the two eighth notes to show ♪♪. The point can be made in dramatic fashion by asking a student to cut the beam connecting a pair of paper eighth notes.

Next, ask the children to notate a series of eight separated eighth notes (♪♪♪♪♪♪♪♪) on the blackboard. You might erase the noteheads and ask the class to clap the series as if the noteheads were still present (↑ ↑ ↑ ↑ ↑ ↑ ↑ ↑).

Holding a paper eighth note without a notehead, flip it so that the tail is reversed (↑). This sign approximates the symbol for the eighth-note rest, which you should then ask the children to write. The class will enjoy performing the eighth note series now substituting rests for one or more of the eighth notes.

Your students are now ready to sing *Entendez Vous*, which begins with an eighth rest. If you teach the song with a quarter note at the beginning and later change it to ⁷, the class will have a graphic aural illustration of the importance of the eighth rest. Your students can also highlight the rest if they walk the beat.

Entendez Vous

French Canon

En - ten-dez vous le ca - ril - lon, der-ry don don

don don don don don don don don.

Good News is another melody which begins with an eighth rest. Have your children write the rhythm of the first two measures after they have learned to sing the song.

Good News

Spiritual/arr. JF

V

Good news char-iots com-in', good news, char-iots com-in',

G

AX

X

BX

good news   char-iots com - in',   don't leave me   be - hind.

4 Perform syncopated rhythm pattern ♪ ♩ ♪

A feeling for the underlying division of the pulse is a prerequisite to accurate performance of syncopation and its relatives, dotted rhythms. Movement activities are a good point of departure, for children can really feel accent displacement when they are moving. Ask the children to walk and clap the beat simultaneously. Now continue to clap the beat but step the beat division. Then ask the children to clap the after-beat (ᵧ ♪) while stepping the beat division. Finally, arrange a series of, say, eight claps on the beat followed by as many off the beat. The 'battle of the beats' takes place when one group claps on, and another off, the beat.

I like to begin notation experience by having the class clap a series of four eighth-notes. They next add ties between any two of the four notes and clap the resulting patterns.

Your students should be able to write these patterns in another way: ♪♪♩, ♩ ♪♪ and ♪♩ ♪. Now introduce the term 'syncopation' to describe the last rhythmic figure. The class will have no difficulty finding this figure in *Do Lord*. In fact this joyous song provides excellent opportunities for practice. You might ask the students to step the song rhythm or to substitute clapping for singing on the syncopated measures. It's also fun to sing only the syncopated measures aloud or to keep the beat with the feet while clapping the quarter note of the syncopated figures (on the word 'Lord'). Still another challenge is to find the syncopation in the seventh measure. Obviously, this lively spiritual is a game in itself.

160

Do Lord

Traditional

Do Lord, oh do Lord, oh do re-mem-ber me,

Do Lord, oh do Lord, oh do re-mem-ber me, Do Lord, oh do Lord, oh

do re-mem-ber me, Look a - way be - yond the blue.

After these introductory activities have been completed, your students should be able to read the syncopated pattern at sight in a variety of contexts.

Next, invite the children to write an original eight-beat phrase which contains the syncopated figure for the class to play. Two of these phrases may be performed in sequence as a B section for *Solas Market* (p.162). Ask the students to find the number of times the syncopated figure occurs in this piece as you sing it for them.

Syncopation in the context of a different rhythmic phrase (♪♩ ♪ | ♫♩) is found in *Lelia* (p.163).

Improvisation activities will help you determine the degree to which your students have assimilated the syncopation pattern. Ask them to create their own eight-beat rhythmic phrases which include the syncopated motive only once. A possible outcome might be: ♩ ♩ ♪♩ ♪♩ ♫♩ ♩ ≀. A further challenge is to incorporate this motive into a sixteen-beat rhythmic improvisation.

5 Read, write, sing, and play dotted quarter-note rhythm patterns ♩. ♪ and ♪ ♩.

In the last lesson your students approached syncopation through the division

161

Solas Market

Calypso/JF

Le-wee go down, Le-wee go down,

Le-wee go down to So - las Mar - ket, Le-wee go down,

Le-wee go down, Le-wee go buy ba - na - na.

Lelia

American/JF

of the beat; now dotted notes are presented in the same manner. Movement again helps the students to internalize the patterns before they encounter notation. Ask the class to clap the quarter-note beat and its division; step once on each group of two clapped eighth notes. Now suggest that they think in sets of four eighth notes; the first step will be held for three claps and the second for only one. When this is secure reverse the note values in the feet. The class will now be ready to step patterns such as ♩. ♪♩. ♪♩ ♩ ♩ ♩ and ♪♩. ♪♩. ♩ ♩ ♩ ♩ while you play on a drum.

A visual breakdown of the rhythmic content of these figures may also help the students to perform them accurately. Have the class first clap, then step ♪♪♪♪. Add ties between two notes as introduced in the previous sequence step (♩♪♪♪). Then ask whether it might be possible to tie three notes together (♪♪♪♪). After the students have clapped and stepped the motive several times, the notation is altered to ♩ ♪♪. The dot is then presented as a substitute for ♪. At this point the clever teacher will remind the children that in the third level they learned that the dot replaced the ♩ (♩.). The temporary confusion can be eliminated with a definition: the dot adds half of the value of the note it follows.

The children can practice the figure just introduced by clapping it in a variety of rhythmic contexts. Some possibilities are:

Students should also be encouraged to invent original eight-beat phrases which include the ♩. ♪ motive.

There are two very good reasons for exploring *Liza Jane* at this point. The refrain contains the syncopated rhythmic motive which the children have recently encountered as well as the new dotted figure just introduced (♩. ♪). When they have learned the melody they should be asked to identify which of the rhythm phrases introduced above represents the refrain of *Liza Jane* (#3).

♪ ♩. is efficiently taught as the reverse of ♩. ♪. *Liza Jane* provides a convenient text illustration of this idea. The children first speak ♩. ♪ ♩ ♩ as they learned it in the song. Then they reverse the note values of the first measure: ♪ ♩. ♩ ♩. After echo clapping a few four-beat patterns which

Liza Jane

American/ arr. JF

include the motive, the students will be ready to encounter it in a song. In preparation for *Sit Down Sister* the students say:

♪ ♩. ⁷ ⁷ | ⁷ ♪ ♩. ⁷ :‖
Sit down   sit down

Now ask the students to sing *Sit Down Sister* (p.167), clapping the rhythmic figure ♪ ♩. wherever it occurs in the song. They will inevitably want to clap on 'sister' but if you notate the rhythm of the first measure the class will see the reason for its omission.

♪ ♩.   ♪ ♩ ♪
sit down sister, I

At this point, students need ways to practice the rhythmic motive they've just learned. I have found two useful approaches; for instance, have your class silently sing the song but clap or step the ♪ ♩. figure; another possibility is to have the students step the beat and clap the figure when it occurs in the melody. And, of course, there are other activities you may design to meet the same end.

Sightreading a variety of rhythm patterns in which the figure is present is another important step in skill development.

Your children will probably recognize the second pattern as the rhythm from the song they have just learned (*Sit Down Sister*).

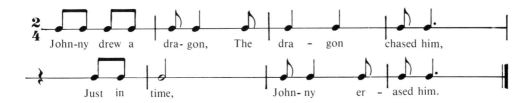

John-ny drew a dra-gon, The dra - gon chased him, Just in time, John-ny er - ased him.

The above rhyme affords another opportunity to perform the ♪ ♩. figure. Try teaching it by rote to encourage aural recognition of the motive. Next, distribute cards, each bearing one measure of the rhythm, to your students; ask them to represent the text rhythm. Now ask the class to reorder the cards to develop a new rhythm to complement the original one. For example:

166

Sit Down Sister

Spiritual/arr. JF

Original rhythm

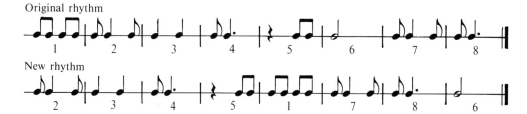

New rhythm

Your class should then perform the composition as a two-part piece or in four groups as a double canon (the second voice enters on the fifth beat in each part). I also regularly ask my students to invent and perform original eight-beat rhythmic phrases which include ♪♩. because these additional activities are excellent ways to reinforce the skill.

6 Take rhythmic dictation: eight- and twelve-beat patterns using all learned note values

The 'Big Ears Game' introduced in second grade and revised in third appears again in a slightly different form to measure rhythmic progress of your fourth-grade students. The form now looks like this.

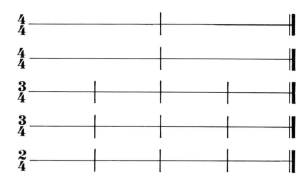

Rhythms appropriate for this level are:

I like to add one extra line for the student's original creations. They are encouraged to write something they can perform for and teach to their classmates.

168

My children find these early exercises very useful before we move to longer phrases. I also find it sensible to avoid mixing a variety of disparate rhythmic motives in the beginning stages. Forms for more advanced stages should include lines for sixteen beats.

7 Read, write, sing, and play pieces beginning with up-beats. Conduct up-beats

Students must understand the term 'down-beat' before the anacrusis or 'up-beat' is introduced. Since the down-beat is obvious in the duple meter conducting pattern, I find it helpful to ask the students to conduct while singing songs about their female friends in duple meter: *Liza Jane* and *Lelia*.

To illustrate the reason for using up-beats I use a simple song like *Come Follow*. I introduce it without text, then have it sung with syllables, accents misplaced.

Now ask your students to speak the text.

> Come follow me to the greenwood tree
> Come follow, follow me.

Add the text to the melody, asking the class whether it felt the same as when spoken. It will be clear that the accents are different and that the bar lines must be shifted to agree with the word accents. The correct version is:

For Health and Strength is another example of a language accent which occurs after the first word. After your children have sung the canon as written, ask them to try it without an up-beat, to test the importance of appropriate word stress in songs.

For Health and Strength

Ging Gong Goolie affords the opportunity to review the sixteenth-note pattern and the newly encountered anacrusis.

Ging Gong Goolie

British Guiana/JF

Ging gong   goo-lie goo-lie goo-lie goo-lie wat-cha, ging gong goo, ging gong goo, ging gong

Several days after you have taught the song and accompaniment distribute cards notated with one beat of its rhythm among eight children.

Ask every other person to stand while the rest kneel; the class claps the standing beats slightly louder than the kneelers. When the children recognize the *Ging Gong* rhythm, the point will be obvious that the song begins with an unaccented beat. The pick-up note leaves the end of the line and kneels to the right of the first accented beat.

Melody

1 Add fa *in the key of F. Recognize the need for the flatted fourth scale degree*

At this point we offer a preliminary introduction to the whole- and half-step composition of the diatonic scale. Begin by having your class review the first phrase of the canon *Chairs to Mend* (Grade Three, p.140) in the keys of G and C. Next, have the students write the first three notes of the song in each key on the staff, locate them on the keyboard charts and, finally, play them on bar instruments.

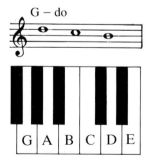

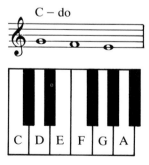

170

The students should now locate *do* on F, writing the first three notes of the song as before.

They will immediately realize that it doesn't sound right when they try it on bar instruments. To understand why, have them compare the keyboard chart of F with those of C and G, checking the order of white and black keys on each.

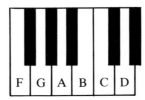

After the children have identified the whole and half steps in each chart, they will recognize that the second note in F-*do* sounded wrong because it was a half, not a whole step. Adding a B-flat bar corrects the interval and prepares the way for the future introduction of key signatures. Adding a B-flat to the three-note score reinforces the concept.

At this point you may wish to introduce a memory aid to help the students remember the diatonic scale intervals they have learned. One such is offered here, with apologies to the Muses.

> Whole steps all would be a bore
> So there's a half between three and four

The first phrase of *Entendez Vous* (introduced on p.159) provides an opportunity to review the concept of the flatted fourth in the F diatonic scale. The canon is purposely scored without a key signature; the children may remember that they must add a B-flat because *do* is located on F. If they don't, you should ask one of the students to play the phrase on a xylophone and the class will discover the error.

A new rhythmic challenge for your class will be to walk the quarter-note beats while singing the canon. Two or more groups may walk anywhere in the room while singing. They must return to the point of departure by the first beat of the last measure.

2 *Add* ti *to the tonal vocabulary in C and F*

Swan Song

When the swan sings   loo   loo   loh,   Loo loo   loh,   loo loo   loh.
Then   my heart is   full of   woe,   Full of   woe,   full of   woe.

The *Swan* canon is a pleasant way to introduce *ti* to your students, thereby completing the diatonic scale and their tonal vocabulary. I have the class learn the song by rote. Then the students sing the melody in syllables from notation; this is the moment to point out *ti*. The children next sing the melody using note names from the keyboard chart.

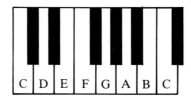

They will find the new half-step interval for themselves. To help them remember what they've just discovered, you might offer this bit of doggerel.

> Our scale's complete! We now locate
> Another half step between seven and eight.

My students like to play the *Swan* canon on bar instruments using contrasting timbre (metal/wood) or registers (soprano/alto). Now have the class perform the canon again, this time transposing *do* to F. Check the F-*do* keyboard chart before playing in this key.

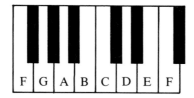

When you ask your students to identify the half steps they will find them between four and five and seven and eight. You might remind them that they must lower the fourth degree by adding a flat to correct the interval between steps three and four of the scale.

172

Music Shall Live provides another opportunity to sing a diatonic melody based on F. Because the practice is necessary, I ask the class to sight-sing individual motives before singing the entire melody.

Measures five through ten may be taught as a sequence: a two-bar motive sung a whole step lower on each repetition.

Then transfer motive 2 (C D E F) to alto glockenspiels; again, the practice is beneficial. Next, reverse the order of the notes and play the pattern in descending fashion as indicated in the score. When your students add the AM and BX parts the end result is a class performance of a three-part canon with instrumental accompaniment.

Music Shall Live

mus - ic a - lone shall live, ne - ver to die.

3 Recognize the need for the raised seventh scale degree (ti) in the key of G

Calypso/arr. JF

All day, all night, Ma - ry Ann, _____
All the lit tle children love Ma - ry Ann, _____

Ma - ry, Ma - ry, Ma - ry Ma - ry Ann,

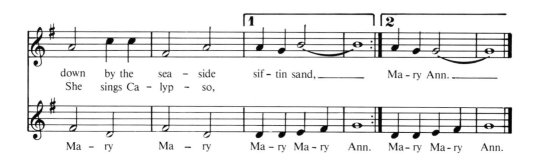

down by the sea - side sif - tin sand, _____ Ma - ry Ann. _____
She sings Ca - lyp - so,

Ma - ry Ma - ry Ma - ry Ma - ry Ann. Ma - ry Ma - ry Ann.

After your children have learned to sing *Mary Ann* in two parts in the key of G, ask a student to play the third and fourth measures of the second voice on an alto xylophone. G

F

E

D

When the wrong note is discovered, the students might be reminded that a keyboard chart has been useful in establishing whole- and half-step intervals on previous occasions. Here is the chart I use for G-*do*.

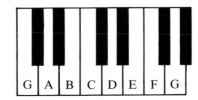

Your students will identify the half-steps occurring between steps three and four and six and seven. In order to create the necessary half-step between seven and eight we must raise the seventh degree by adding a sharp.

The students may now try the *Swan* canon on the instruments in G-*do*. They will quickly find that a raised seventh degree is necessary to correct the mixolydian sound created by the F-natural.

4 Write key signatures in C, F, and G diatonic

At this point it is important for the class to review the interval construction of the diatonic scale beginning on C; use a keyboard chart to simplify matters. As the identical whole- and half-step arrangements are transferred to F-*do* and G-*do*, ask the students to add the accidental appropriate to each key. Next, introduce the key signature as a means of identifying *do* thereby avoiding the addition of chromatic alterations throughout the score.

After this rationale for key signatures has been established, teach your class the typical means of finding *do* from the key signature.

Texture

1 Sing three- and four-part diatonic canons

Lullaby

We all know that practice is always important and especially so with sightreading. Hence the use of the full diatonic scale makes the *Lullaby* canon a good exercise for students. *Lullaby* also lends itself to canon performance on bar instruments and it should be transposed to the keys of F and G. My students always make up new words for this canon.

The canons which follow may be taught by rote or note. *Every Sleeper* can be performed in canon on unpitched percussion instruments. Parts of *Ah Poor Bird* and *Strawberries* are good for melodic interval practice and for the experience of holding a part in ensemble performance.

Ho! Every Sleeper Waken

Ho, ev'- ry sleep-er wak - en, the sun is in the sky! Come
rise,_____ Come rise,_____ and hear the cuck-oo cry. Cuck -
oo! Cuck - oo! Wake up! Be spry!

Ah Poor Bird

1. Ah poor bird, take your flight, Far a-bove the sor- rows of this sad night.
2. Ah poor bird, as you fly, Can you see the dawn of to - mor-row's sky?

Strawberries

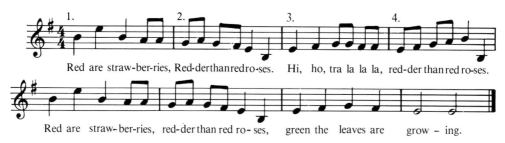

Red are straw-ber-ries, Red-der than red ro-ses. Hi, ho, tra la la la, red-der than red ro-ses.
Red are straw-ber-ries, red-der than red ro-ses, green the leaves are grow - ing.

2 Sing chord roots and play pieces requiring a I-V harmonic setting on bar instruments

Students at this level are introduced to functional harmony through bass movement from the bordun to the octave based on the fifth scale degree.

My children enjoy experimenting with a variety of given I-V patterns while I improvise on the recorder. Some examples are:

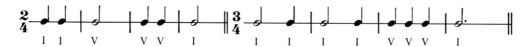

You might then isolate the following pattern.

176

This is the bass xylophone part for the instrumental piece that follows. You or an able student may perform the recorder melody.

Instrumental Piece

JF

The chord pattern learned above may be applied to *Go Tell Aunt Rhody*. In this score, however, the part is divided between the bass xylophone and the alto xylophone. The recorder countermelody might be used as a sight-singing exercise before it is added to the ensemble. Try performing the piece in the keys of both G and F.

Go Tell Aunt Rhody

Trad./JF

Improvisation

1 Create instrumental introductions, codas, and contrasting sections for song material

This step in the sequence gives your class a chance to review some of the material learned during the year and to extend those pieces with improvised sections. *Go Tell Aunt Rhody* might be introduced with a four-bar dominant pedal and the recorder or glockenspiel playing a simple rhythmic figure on a few pitches. Here is an example.

Your class will suggest many other ideas.

Listening

1 Perform and listen to examples of chaconne

Orff students have been working with ostinato patterns combined in contrapuntal style throughout their school experience. Now they have an opportunity to see how these elements are applied in a larger-scale work — the chaconne. The following student example is adapted from *In Canon* to give students the idea of the structure. Parts should be layered from the bottom up, as indicated by the numbers in the score.[1] Note that parts two and three offer students a chance to review the structure of the diatonic scale. The relationship of this piece to the popular Pachelbel Canon is a delightful discovery for my students.

Purcell Canon for Instruments

178

Another example of this form written for recorders, but playable on bar instruments, may be found in Volume V of *Music for Children* (Murray, Schott Edition 10920), p. 61. You may select from many Bach, Handel, and Purcell examples for related listening.[2]

9 · Grade Five: Towards Independent Musicianship

Your class brings a broad range of abilities to this fifth year of instruction. Given sufficient amounts of time, effort, and aptitude, the majority of your students will be reasonably proficient in performing rhythms convergent with and divergent from the beat. They will also be able to read and write music in three major keys. In addition, their technical skills with Orff instruments will have improved immensely over the years as will their ability to move and sing. These skills are the foundation for the five goals that shape the content of this year's work.

1. The class encounters new and more complex rhythmic challenges; the dotted notes, rests, and syncopation learned in Grade Four are now reduced by half. Then the beat unit is changed from quarter to eighth notes. Lastly, students perform and listen to pieces with irregular phrase-length construction.

2. Our second focus is melody: the *la* tonal center is reviewed and the class now performs music in the aeolian mode. This is the first time your students will sing, play, and improvise in the full minor scale.

3. A new texture is our third goal. To this point all part singing has been contrapuntal. Now your class is introduced to two-voice singing in parallel motion. This new skill is then applied in subsequent stages of this year's work. Then your students return to contrapuntal style but this time the music is more complex. A second harmonic challenge for the students will be to provide three-chord accompaniments for their melodies. As with all of the work in this chapter, it is an elaboration of what has gone before. In Grade Four two-chord accompaniments were introduced; now a third is added. Since much of the music of our culture is based on the I-IV-V chord progression it is essential that literate students be able to use and understand it.

4. Our fourth goal centers on improvisation. As usual, these exercises give your students a chance to use in new ways the musical skills they have acquired. At this level these abilities should lead to freer, more open-ended responses to improvisation problems than in the past.

5. We conclude with the customary listening exercise designed to both review past work while linking it to music beyond the performance capabilities of the class. In this case, as in Grade Four, we focus on the chaconne. Here the emphasis is on rhythmic variations and contrasts between major and minor, two principal themes in this year's work.

Below are the goals and the learning sequence to achieve them.

Rhythm

1 Read, write, sing, and play songs and instrumental pieces using ♩♫ , ♫♩ , ♫♫ and ♪

2 Change the beat unit to eight. Perform rhythm and bar instrument pieces in $\frac{4}{8}$ and $\frac{3}{8}$ meters

3 Read, write, sing, and play pieces in $\frac{6}{8}$ meter

Melody

1 Identify *la* tonal center in diatonic material (aeolian mode)

Texture

1 Sing and play pieces using parallel thirds and sixths

2 Sing chord roots and play on bar instruments pieces requiring a I-IV-V harmonic setting

3 Perform three- and four-voice canons with accompaniment

4 Perform pieces with three independent voice parts

Rhythm II

1 Perform and listen to pieces with irregular phrase length construction

Improvisation

1 Improvise pieces with bar and other instruments employing expressive contrasts

Listening

1 Perform, create, and listen to examples of theme and variations form

Rhythm

1 Read, write, sing, and play songs and instrumental pieces using ♫♩, ♩♫., ♫♫ and ♪

I like to prepare students for sixteenth-note syncopation, dotted rhythms, and rests in ways that closely resemble the presentation of similar eighth-note figures in Grade Four. Have the class review the familiar sixteenth-note pattern ♬♬ by saying 'coca cola' (or any other word or combination of four syllables you or your class select) while patting the beat. A student may be asked to notate this figure. Then tie different combinations of adjacent notes such as ♬♬ or ♬♬ and ask the class to say and clap the resulting sound: ♪ ♪ co-co and ♪ ♪ ♪ co-ca--la . Students will surely remember other possible combinations of tied notes which they have learned: ♬♬ ♬♬ ♬♬ ♬♬
co-cola   coca co-   co--la   coca--

Notation of these patterns follows the procedure previously introduced in writing dotted eighth-note and syncopated patterns.

1 ♬♬ is written ♫ ♩

2 ♬♬♬ is written ♩ ♫♫

3 ♬♬♬ is written ♫♫ ♩

Now slowly lead your class through the following steps.

4 ♫♫ is written ♫ ♩

5 ♫♫ is written ♫♩ then ♪ ♪

6 ♫♫ is written ♩♫ then ♪ ♪

My own procedure is to offer a variety of rhythmic examples to perform on body and unpitched percussion as well as song literature containing each rhythm figure. Students also need many opportunities to write original four- and eight-beat phrases including these patterns.

It is crucial that students have opportunities to compare dotted quarter- and dotted eighth-note rhythms through performance. For example, they might be asked to clap ♩. ♪♩ ♩ then ♪ ♪♪♪ while keeping the beat with their feet. Or they might perform the following rhythmic phrases in succession.

Analysis of dotted notes and syncopated figures in each phrase provides a basis for comparison of the two phrases. Students may wish to substitute figures from one of the phrases for another after they can successfully perform the pieces as written. For instance, the third and fourth beats in the first measure of each phrase may be exchanged, with the following result:

Dotted eighth notes and the syncopated figure ♫♩ are emphasized in the song material that follows.

The rhythmic figure ♩♩ predominates in *Caimarusa*, a folk song from Columbia. Notating the subdivision of the beat helps assure accuracy in the performance of the melody of the chorus.

Caimarusa

Folk Song from Columbia/arr. JF

Cai-ma, Cai-ma, Cai-ma-ru-sa, Cai-ma - ru - sa, Cai-ma-ru - sa, Cai-ma,

Cai-ma, Cai-ma-ru - sa, Cai-ma - ru - sa sa!

La la la_____ la la la la_____ la la la

La la la la la, la la la,

la_____ la la la la, La la la_____ la la la

la la la, la la la, la la la,

la_____ la la la la_____ la la la la!

la la la, la la la la la la la la la!

♫., the reverse of the rhythmic figure explored immediately above, is well represented in the following West Indies song.[1] The melody is so constructed that the motive ♫. ♪ or ♫. ♩ occurs every other measure. Have your students clap two beats of sixteenth notes (♬ ♬) followed by the dotted motive to practice the underlying subdivision. They will discover other dotted patterns as they become acquainted with the melody.

Bassez Down

West Indian Folk Song/arr. BK

Bas - sez, ma ma, Bas-sez down, Bas-sez in the morn-ing, Bas-sez down, Bas -

Bas-sez down Bas-sez down, mis-sie Ma - ry, Bas-sez down, Bas-sez down, mis-sie Ma - ry,

Bas-sez down, Bas-sez down, mis-sie Ma-ry, Bas-sez down, Bas-sez in the morn-ing, Bas-sez down.

Clapping is good preparation for performance of the motive found in *Boomba.*[2] This is the rhythmic material of the odd-numbered bars and the last four measures of the song.

The rest is introduced in the context of a series of sixteenth notes (). A necessary preliminary step to introducing the rest is to separate these notes: . The notehead is erased and the flag reversed to introduce . The glockenspiel part of *Amapola la Creola* offers an opportunity for practice. You might count the first measure of this part as ; then illustrate it and, finally . The two-measure ostinato pattern should be written to give your students practice in internalizing subdivisions of the beat. My inclination is to delay introducing the parallel voice below the melody until later (p.199).

Boomba

Brazilian/arr. JF

Bring out the big bull Boom – ba

Sam-ba and Mam-ba Boom – ba, Boom-ba la Boom-ba la la la la la, Boom-ba la Boom-ba

la la   la la la,   Sam-ba and Mam- ba,   Boom-ba   la Bam - ba   jump like a jam – ba

Boom-ba   la Bam - ba.

Slowly fading away, without ritardando.

187

Amapola la Creola

Rural Samba/Brazil arr. JF

Am-a - po - la la la Cre - o - la, learned to play the bass vi - o - la, But
sev-en or eight years lat - er, Gave it up for the vic - tro - la!

2. Fly a jet plane sola
   Ended up at the North Pola!
3. Ordered Swiss cheese with a hola
   She was served a Coca-Cola!
4. Out of work and on the dola
   Took a cruise to East Angola!

Your students will want to use the rhythmic patterns they have encountered this year in improvising new pieces. Here are the patterns.

Caimarusa:

Bassez down:

Boomba:

These motives may be used singly or in sequence in developing rhythmic phrases for performance on percussion or bar instruments.

2 Change beat unit to eight. Perform rhythm and bar instrument pieces in $\frac{4}{8}$ and $\frac{3}{8}$ meters

This step in the sequence is an important prerequisite to the introduction of $\frac{6}{8}$ meter. I introduce the concept of changing the beat unit by demonstrating that the bottom, as well as the top, number in the meter signature may change. When your children understand that any note value may serve as the beat unit (meters written with the note values instead of numbers help to illustrate this idea: ) they are ready to proceed with the activities that follow.

Speech again helps to introduce this concept. After the students can say:

> Psycapoo the silly goose
> Brushed his teeth with carrot juice

ask them to write it in four measures of $\frac{4}{4}$ meter.

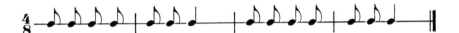

Now have your children change the beat unit to eight and ask them to notate the poem to fit the new meter.

Next, have the students step eighth notes as they clap and speak the poem. After this is successfully accomplished they may step quarter notes while clapping and speaking the poem.

At this point I find it helpful to test understanding of the concept by asking my class to perform the following rhythm canon on two contrasting percussion instruments.

In a follow-up exercise the students might be asked to demonstrate their understanding of $\frac{4}{8}$ meter by providing the necessary bar lines for the rhythm canon.

$\frac{3}{8}$ meter may also be introduced through the medium of speech. Many students will know the proverb: Red sky at night, sailor's de-light. Before they are ask to try to notate it in $\frac{3}{8}$ meter, they should be asked to guess the kind of single note that fills a whole measure in this meter (♩.). After your students have notated *Red Sky* ask them to perform one or both voices of the following rhythm composition.

Three Little Pigs is an example of an authentic folk melody written in $\frac{3}{8}$ meter. My class enjoys clapping the rhythms of both voices, although they are too sophisticated to take the text seriously.

Three Little Pigs

American/arr. JF

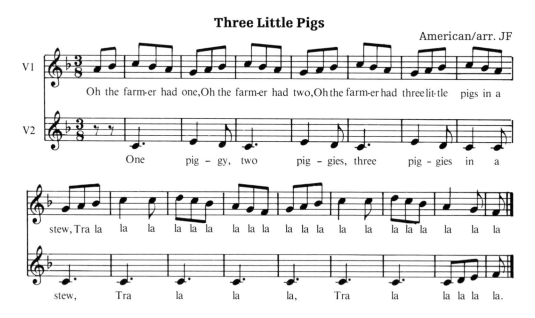

The following English piece in $\frac{3}{8}$ is well within the competence of fifth-level singers and players.

190

Go Merrily

English/arr. JF

A shift from $\frac{4}{8}$ to $\frac{3}{8}$ is illustrated by the following version of the *Grand Old Duke*. Children should pat-clap to accompany their singing on the $\frac{4}{8}$ section and pat during the $\frac{3}{8}$ part. It is possible that your children performed this in the primary grades, walking forward and back on the first section and following two leaders who make arches through which all subsequent couples pass during the section in triple meter.

Grand Old Duke (I)

I have often been surprised by student requests to play games learned years earlier in their school experience, but if they choose not to play, they've already become conscious of meter contrasts, the purpose of this piece.

3 Read, write, sing, and play pieces in $\frac{6}{8}$ meter

The irony of $\frac{6}{8}$ meter is that for all of its notation complications, it is in the speech and games of very young American children. The skip is a triple locomotor movement and many nursery rhymes are in $\frac{6}{8}$ meter. The song *Throw It Out the Window* uses this heritage in a humorous way.

Throw it Out the Window

Lit-tle Miss Muf - fet   sat on a tuf - fet   eat-ing her Christ-mas   pie, ___   a -

long came a spi-der and   sat down be-side her, she   threw him out   the   win-dow. ___   The

win-dow, ___   the   win-dow, ___   the   sec - ond sto - ry   win-dow. ___   A -

long came a spi-der and   sat down be-side her, she   threw him out   the   win-dow. ___

(Use other nursery rhymes for texts.)

Students should also have the opportunity to feel the $\frac{6}{8}$ meter in movement. Older students can be motivated to skip if it is presented as part of a sequence with walking or jumping, as in this example.

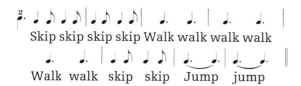

Skip skip skip skip Walk walk walk walk

Walk walk skip skip Jump jump

Students should be encouraged to develop their own sequences and to accompany them with percussion instruments. These activities prepare your class for the notation of this new meter.

Children who understand the principle of changing beat unit are ready for at least one of the complications of $\frac{6}{8}$ time. The next step is to have your children explore the multitude of rhythmic variations possible within this meter. My approach begins with each student composing a $\frac{6}{8}$ measure. Then I select three or four and organize them into a four-measure phrase for the class to learn. An example might be:

Another version of the *Grand Old Duke* and a new composition, *Oats, Peas, Beans* provide further opportunities for singing and playing $\frac{6}{8}$ meter material.

Grand Old Duke (II)

Trad./arr. JF

Oats Peas Beans

Trad./arr. JF

Following these activities, your children should be ready for rhythmic dictation in $\frac{6}{8}$ meter. Two measures are sufficient at first, though students will soon want to try longer examples.

Melody

1 Identify la tonal center in diatonic material (aeolian mode)

Your students were preparing for the minor mode when they worked with *la* centered pentatonic material in Grade Three (see pp.134-137). The minor is introduced now as the *la* scale was then, in relationship to *do*. The students first sing the major diatonic scale with syllables, then play it on instruments. Next, they sing and play it again, this time beginning on *la*. Now you identify the scale as the aeolian mode, the natural version of the minor scale. Our first example, the *Aeolian Lullaby* may be taught in two-measure segments; the class will enjoy arranging them in the correct order.

Aeolian Lullaby

American/arr. JF

V: Go to sleep-y ba – by, loo loo loo loo loo,

Close your eyes and go to sleep, while I sing to you.

The canons which follow may be performed by two recorder players together with drummers selected from the class. You might contrast the sounds of major and minor by playing each melody in its parallel major key.

Canon for Alto Recorders and Drum

JF

Canon for Soprano Recorder and Drum[3]

G Keetman

Finally, is a lovely old American carol for recorders to play or voices to sing on loo. The spare accompaniment encourages vocal improvisation in the aeolian mode.

Lullay My Liking

American/arr. JF

Texture

1 Sing and play pieces using parallel thirds and sixths

So far your students have done only contrapuntal part-singing; two or more voices have been combined in imitative or independent fashion. The next challenge is imitative movement parallel to the melody – sometimes called paraphony. The pull of one voice to another in homophonic vocal style makes it the most difficult kind of part singing; student success is therefore much greater when these complexities are delayed to this point.

In the early stages of parallel vocal work, I like to have the class begin on a unison pitch and find the higher or lower third from that tone. The second voice of *I'm Gonna Walk the Streets* illustrates a stepwise approach to the sixth below the melody in the fourth bar. The addition of the independent ostinato third voice thickens the texture to the extent that the only instrument part added is a bass to support the voices.

I'm Gonna Walk the Streets

Spiritual/arr. JF

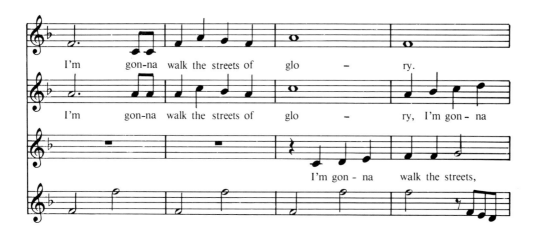

Walk the streets of glo - ry one of these days.____

walk the streets of glo - ry one of these days, one of these days.

I'm gon - na walk the streets.

You will recall that parallel thirds were scored for both the voice and xylophone parts of *Amapola la Creola*. I find it useful to teach the second voice part of *Amapola* and to review the xylophone parallel thirds at this point.

2 Sing chord roots and play on bar instruments pieces requiring a I-IV-V harmonic setting

You will very likely find it useful to review the two-chord material introduced in Grade Four before presenting pieces requiring the subdominant chord accompaniment. Students have not yet been required to determine chord changes by ear; now they should be asked to provide the bass chord root accompaniment for the familiar *Go Tell Aunt Rhody* and other two-chord songs without your assistance. Because only one class member can perform on the bass, you will need to find a way to have all of the students demonstrate competence in hearing implied chord changes. One of my solutions is to have the children close their eyes while singing a familiar melody; they then use their hands to indicate when the chords should change. These are the signs.

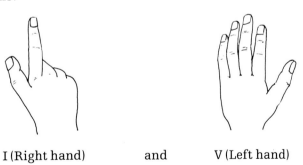

I (Right hand)   and   V (Left hand)

You may choose to present the more demanding challenge of asking the class to sing chord roots while an unfamiliar melody is played or sung. Here is a melody which you might use.

The next challenge is to provide a melody for a given bass. One of the sample bass lines offered for this purpose is in *Music for Children*, American Edition (Vol. III, p. 130).

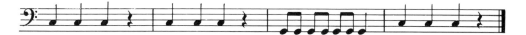

Students must be given much careful preparation in improvising melodies with implied chord changes. Here are some steps which you might take to help them succeed.

Students play (sing) *two* notes which may be used with the I chord

Students may play (sing) these *two* notes only when they hear the tonic in the bass

Students play (sing) *two* notes which may be used with the V chord

Students may play (sing) these *two* notes only when they hear the dominant in the bass

Only after successfully performing I and V separately may the entire bass line be decorated

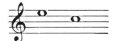

I notes for melody

V notes for melody

Here is one of the many possible results of this exercise.

If the class is ready to be stretched further, you might add the *third* tone for each of the two chords. Adding passing notes on weak beats is the final step in improvising melodies over a two-chord accompaniment. Once the students have mastered these tasks they are ready for the introduction of the subdominant chord.

Listening to 'Gassenhauer' from the recording *Street Song* (Quintessence 7127) is one means of acquainting the students with the sounds of tonic, dominant and subdominant chords in context. You may help the class to follow the chord changes by giving them a *Street Song* chord map.

Road Map for Street Song

I	I	IV	IV

I	I	V	V

I	I	IV	IV

I	V	I	I

IV	V	I	I

IV	V	I	I

My approach is to ask students to sing chord roots and to play the bass line along with the recording. They invariably want to try to play at least part of the piece themselves.[4]

The four-measure ostinato bass line in *Wimoweh* is a rare example of a repeated I-IV-I-V progression and it is easy for the students to master because of this regularity. They should sing it with syllables before transferring it to bar instruments. Voice two is added next, then the glockenspiel, followed by the first voice melody. Parts may be added to or deleted from the performance as seems wise. The bass continues throughout as well as the conga, bongo, maracas, and other color parts which you or the class may add.

Wimoweh

Traditional S. African/adapted JF

V1: In the jun-gle the qui - et jun-gle the li - on sleeps to - night,_____

V2: Ooo_____ wi-mo-weh.

* Voice 3. sings *Wimoweh* throughout

In *Bahia Town* is a more typical song requiring a I-IV-V setting because it is not based on a repeated chord sequence. You might assign two different groups of students the responsibility for accompanying the two sections of the piece. Other suggestions for developing I-IV-V chord changes are offered in pp. 165-6 of *Music for Children*, American Edition, Volume III.

In Bahia Town

Brazilian/arr. JF

In Ba - hi - a   far a-way, the   co - co-nuts fall   down.

3 Perform three- and four-voice canons with accompaniment

You may choose to perform this beautiful canon without accompaniment. A bit of color, however, has been provided here to support the voices. This example illustrates that canon accompaniments must be spare in texture and scored, for the most part, below the voice parts.

Kyrie

Trad./arr. JF

Ky - ri - e,   ky - ri - e,   e - lei - son.

Ky - ri - e,   ky - ri - e,   e - lei - son.

Ky - ri - e,   ky - ri - e,   e - lei - son.

4 Perform pieces with three independent voice parts

Mary Ann, introduced as a two-voice composition in Grade Four, returns as an appropriate example for beginning three-part vocal work. Your students will find little difficulty in performing it successfully because the second voice always begins on a tone sung by the first or third voice part.

Mary Ann

Calypso/arr. JF

Let Us Sing makes much greater demands on your students' musical abilities than does *Mary Ann*. Each voice is independent of the other and the hemiola in the seventh measure provides a rhythmic challenge for all.

Let Us Sing

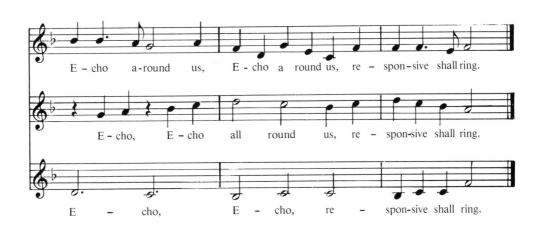

Rhythm II

1 Perform and listen to pieces with irregular phrase length construction

In my experience, students can discover unequal phrase length construction by reviewing the question/answer phrase building device first introduced in Grade Two. After they have tried questions and answers of equal length in different meters, ask them to make the answer shorter or longer than the question. There is no need to be specific about the number of beats or bars to be changed at first; rather, I find it best to let the students experiment with length for themselves. Small groups of students may work out separate answers to a given rhythmic question, each playing their results for the class.

A melodic example which illustrates unequal phrase length is *There Was a Man*, a folk song from Newfoundland.

There Was a Man

Folk Song from Newfoundland

The students will discover the following phrase structure in this song:

Phrase 1   four measures
     2   six measures
     3   four measures
     4   four measures
     5   six measures

A divided class can perform the song to illustrate the unequal phrase lengths; group one sings the four-measure phrases and group two the six. Or the class could clap the rhythm of the four-measure phrases and sing the six.

The four-measure question/six-measure answer idea is nicely illustrated in the minuet of the Haydn String Quartet Op.76 #1. The first ten measures present this arrangement exactly. After it is repeated, a four-measure question is followed by an eight-measure answer. Students enjoy playing musical detective if they are given some clues, such as 'The answer will be longer than the four-measure question. How much longer is it?' The rapid tempo of this movement adds to the listening challenge.

Menuetto from String Quartet Op. 76 No. 1

Haydn

The following composition is intended as an A section for a rondo to be developed and performed by the students.[5] The tympani plays a four-measure question to be answered by six-measure improvisations on membrane (B), wood (C), and metal (D) unpitched percussion instruments.

Ich Spring an Disem Ring

Improvisation

1 Improvise pieces with bar and other instruments employing expressive contrasts

Improvisation at this level can become a means of reviewing expressive, as well as pitch and rhythm, elements. You and your class can develop a variety of pieces based on dynamic, accent, color, and tempo contrasts. One example is the Langston Hughes poem *The City*.[6]

208

In the morning the city
Spreads its wings
Making a song in stone that sings.

In the evening the city goes to bed
Hanging lights above its head.

Your class will have to make decisions about instrumental color appropriate for each verse, considering such possibilities as wood contrasted with metal, percussion contrasted with pitch, and so on. You or a student may improvise a piano solo characterized by tempo and/or dynamic changes; unpitched instruments may supply accents if necessary.

Pieces of this kind are effective with an atonal harmonic setting; this is achieved by using both B flat and F sharp bars. The piano improvisation is free from tonal and rhythmic restrictions, but it must evoke the contrasting moods of the poem.

The Hughes poem is, of course, only one of countless examples. I find it very helpful to ask the class for further suggestions.

Listening

1 Perform, create, and listen to examples of theme and variations form

I have chosen this chaconne to demonstrate variations because the theme is short and the form is clear. In addition, the shift from major to minor in variations nine through sixteen underscores the work in minor undertaken earlier in the year. My outline of a variety of activities developed to demonstrate theme and variations form may be found on pp. 328-331 of Volume III of *Music for Children*, American Edition.[7]

Chaconne from Trois Leçons

Handel

Var. 20

Var. 21

Conclusion

In the introduction to this book we met Rebecca in the midst of discovering the wonderful sounds stored away in a room full of Orff instruments. In the days that followed Rebecca grew quite at a home with glockenspiels and xylophones; in a few more years she will finish the five grades covered in this book. What will she be likely to learn? From a strictly musical point of view Rebecca will acquire a considerable musical vocabulary; she will know much about using sound expressively and her aural comprehension skills will enable her to listen perceptively. The sum of these accomplishments is twofold. First, Rebecca will gain some measure of musical independence. Second, she will experience success and pleasure in these musical encounters thereby deepening her love of music. How much independence and how much love will be determined largely by the amount of intelligence, talent and caring that she, her classmates, and I bring to the task.

But there is also a broader dimension to what Rebecca stands to learn in these early years of her musical education. In an Orff classroom music is a social act. Consequently, Rebecca will be part of a musical community with all that a community entails in the way of sharing and compromising, helping and supporting. She already knows the pleasure of teaching her less accomplished classmates; she also realizes that for all her talent there are others still more gifted.

All of these outcomes are largely the result of very subtle interplay between teacher, learners, content, and method. If we teachers are insensitive it is only too obvious what will happen. The same holds true for Rebecca. But her classmates will also have an impact. If they support and urge her on she will certainly have a more rewarding experience than if they do not; in an important sense they are her teachers too. Finally, content and method have parts to play. Willing teachers and eager students won't accomplish much if the music is banal or, even if glorious, is presented in self-defeating ways. Ideally, what we need is a combination of content and method which not only makes the most of our talent and character but even stirs us on to do more. And that brings us to Orff's legacy. In his combination of media, pedagogy, and theory he provided us with what we need to make the most of music education. I can only hope that this book makes that legacy accessible to you and all your Rebeccas.

What Should You Do Next?

If you are intrigued by the possibilities of Orff practice then your next step is further education. Orff teachers accomplish that in two ways. One form of instruction is carried on by local chapters. There are scores of these and most of them hold one-day workshops several times during the school year. These workshops, which often provide optional graduate credit, commonly meet on Saturday for five or six hours and are taught by the chapter's own most experienced teachers or by guest experts. A typical session might focus on one or two of the following subjects: Orff pedagogy, dance, movement, recorder playing, choral music, vocal development, story telling and drama, or improvisation. In keeping with Orff tradition, there is much emphasis on group participation; those who attend learn by doing.

The best way to find out about these workshops is to contact the Orff chapter nearest you. In the United States, write the Executive Secretary, American Orff-Schulwerk Association, P.O. Box 391089, Cleveland, Ohio 44139-1089, or call 216-543-5366. In Canada write Music for Children/ Musique Pour Enfants: Carl Orff Canada, c/o Faculty of Music, Edward Johnson Building, University of Toronto, Toronto, Canada or call 416-978-3750. In Australia write the Australia National Council of Orff-Schulwerk Associations, PO Box 225, Strathfield, 2135, New South Wales, Australia or call 02-759-6796 or 02-708-2960.

The second important method of education for Orff teachers is through summer courses. These are held in the United States, Canada, and Australia generally for two weeks and focus on all elements of Orff practice. Beginning students enroll in a Level One course and in subsequent summers progress through second and third levels. Master-class opportunities are also available. Again, the best way to learn about such programs is by writing to the various national Orff headquarters at the above addresses. Both the AOSA and Music For Children: Carl Orff Canada offer further services to their members, not the least of which is money for education and/or research in Orff-Schulwerk. For complete details on this and other benefits contact the organizations.

Surely one of the most picturesque of the summer possibilities is in Salzburg, Austria. There, in odd-numbered summers, the Orff Institute hosts a two-week course in English open to anyone interested in Orff practice. More information can be obtained by writing to the Orff Institute, Frohnburgweg 55, A-5020, Salzburg, Austria.

One very important benefit of these two forms of instruction — workshops and summer courses — is the chance to meet and learn from people with interests like your own. Such contacts, especially with people who have much Orff experience, can be helpful and stimulating to the new teacher.

Clearly, your 'next step' includes many possibilities but, whichever you choose, a potentially rich musical and educational experience awaits you.

Notes

1 The Gift and Challenge of Carl Orff

1. This chapter is based on Carl Orff's autobiography, especially Vol.3, *The Schulwerk*, Schott, 1978; Andreas Liess, *Carl Orff*, St Martin's Press, 1966 and Lilo Gersdorf, *Carl Orff*, Rowohlt, 1981.
2. Orff, p.14
3. *ibid.*, p.15
4. *ibid.*, p.67
5. *ibid.*, p.214
6. *ibid.*, p.218

2 Orff Media

1. From a speech delivered at the Royal Conservatory of Music, Toronto, 1962.
2. An excellent outline of Orff media can be found in *Guidelines for Orff-Schulwerk Training Courses*, American Orff-Schulwerk Association, 1980, pp.16-23.
3. Specific lesson plans based on this approach can be found in Frazee and Kreuter, *Sound Ideas*, Musik Innovations, 1984.

3 Orff Pedagogy

1. *Orff Echo*, Vol.XV, Number 3, Spring 1983, p.7.

4 Orff Theory

1. Wilhelm Keller, *Introduction to Music for Children*, Schott, 1963.
2. Carl Orff and Gunild Keetman, *Musik für Kinder*, Vols.I-V, Schott, 1950-54.
3. For elaboration, see Willi Apel, *Harvard Dictionary of Music*, 2nd edition, Harvard University Press, 1969, pp.634-5.
4. *Music for Children*, American Edition, Vol.I, p.22.
5. Carl Orff and Gunild Keetman, *Paralipomena*, Schott, 1977.
6. This useful approach was suggested to me by my colleague and friend, Mary Goetze of Indiana University, who has given her permission to include it in this volume.
7. Carl Orff and Gunild Keetman, *Musik für Kinder*, Schott, 1950, Vol.II, p.9.
8. *ibid.*, p.16.

5 Grade One: Beginning at the Beginning

1. *Music for Children*, American Edition, Vol.I, p.44.
2. *Music for Children*, American Edition, Vol.II, p.4.

3. *ibid.*, p.14.
4. *ibid.*, p.105.
5. *ibid.*, p.191.
6. Aaron, Tossi and Wuytack, Jos, *Joy*, Leduc, Paris, 1972, p.7.
7. *Music for Children*, American Edition, Vol.II, p.125.

7 Grade Three: Extending the Musical Vocabulary

1. *Music for Children*, American Edition, Vol.II, p.182.
2. *ibid.*, p.92.
3. *ibid.*, p.42.
4. *ibid.*, p.68.
5. *ibid.*, p.42.
6. *ibid.*, p.81.
7. *ibid.*, p.133.
8. *ibid.*, p.46.
9. Reprinted from *Ten Folk Carols for Christmas*, Jane Frazee, Schott, 1977, p.6.
10. Suggested recording: Jean-Philippe Rameau, *Pièces de Clavecin*, Albert Fuller, harpsichord (Nonesuch H-71278).

8 Grade Four: Developing Musical Proficiency

1. Bisgaard and Aaron, Magnamusic/ Wm Hansen, 1978.
2. See also Frazee and Kreuter, *Sound Ideas*, Musik Innovations, 1984, Lesson IV.

9 Grade Five: Towards Independent Musicianship

1. Kulich, Birthe, *Method for the Recorder: Windsongs, Book 6* (Empire Music, Vancouver, B.C.), p.53.
2. *Music for Children*, American Edition, Vol.III, pp.201-3.
3. Gunild Keetman, *Stücke, für Flöte und Trommel*, Schott Edition 3625.
4. The score may be found in *Music for Children*, English Adaptation by Margaret Murray, Schott Edition 4867, pp.48-55.
5. Reprinted from Jane Frazee, *Old Music for Young Players*, St Albans Press, 1985.
6. *Music for Children*, American Edition, Vol.III, p.245.
7. See also Frazee and Kreuter, *Sound Ideas*, Musik Innovations, 1984, Lesson V.

Appendices

Ranges of Instruments

Ranges of the Bar Instruments

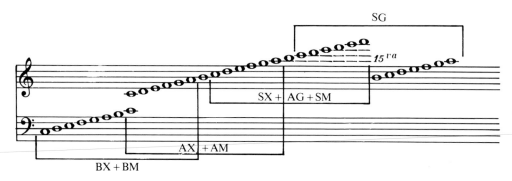

All bar instruments are notated:
(Only AX and AM sound actual notated pitch.)

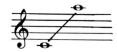

Range of the Recorders

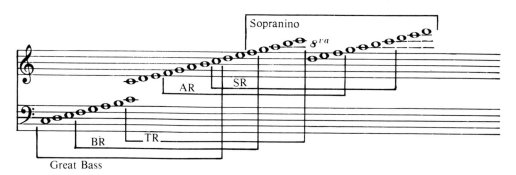

Placement of Instruments on a Score, with Abbreviations and Symbols

S   Voice — Soprano
A   — Alto
T   — Tenor
B   — Bass
SoR   Sopranino Recorder
SR   Soprano Recorder
AR   Alto Recorder
TR   Tenor Recorder
BR   Bass Recorder
SG   Soprano Glockenspiel
AG   Alto Glockenspiel
SX   Soprano Xylophone
AX   Alto Xylophone
SM   Soprano Metallophone
AM   Alto Metallophone

Percussion: Metals

Symbol		Symbol	
△	Triangle	∞	Finger Cymbals
	Jingle Bells		Chime Tree
	Agogo Bells		Cow Bell
	Cymbals		Slide Whistle
	Sistre		Flexi-tone

Percussion: Woods

Symbol		Symbol	
	Wood Block		Tic-toc Block
	Castanets		Shakers
	Maracas		Cabasa
	Ratchet		Rattles
	Temple Blocks		Vibra Slap
X	Claves		Guiro or Reco Reco
	Log Drum		Sand Blocks

Percussion: Membranes or Skins

Symbol		Symbol	
○	Hand Drum		Tambourine
	Bongo Drums		Conga Drum
	Snare Drum		

Large Percussion

Symbol	
	Hanging Cymbal
	Gong
	Bass Drum

G   Guitar
BX   Bass Xylophone
BM   Bass Metallophone
      Tympani
      Piano
      Double Bass

Outline of Musical Skills and Understandings

Grade	Rhythm	Melody	Texture	Harmony	Form
1	♩ ♫ 𝄾	Pentatonic: *l s m r d* (Aural only)	Monophonic Counterpoint	Simple tonic Bordun: chord/level	Motive AA AB
2	(note values) 2/4 4/4 Bar lines	Pentatonic: *d¹ l s m r d* (Aural and written)	Polyphonic (2-part canon) Vocal ostinati	Moving bordun (Two instruments) Three borduns: chord, broken, level	Motive to phrase ABA
3	♩. 3/4	Names of lines/spaces Hexatonic: *d¹ l s f m r d s₁ l₁* *Do* centered pentatonic *La* centered pentatonic G clef	3-part canon	Arpeggiated bordun Moving bordun (One instrument)	Four-bar phrase Repeated phrases Rondo
4	(note values) Syncopation Anacrusis	Diatonic: *d t l s f m r d*	4-part canon	I-V	Chaconne
5	(note values) 3/8 4/8 6/8	Diatonic minor *l s f m r d t₁ l₁*	Paraphony	I-IV-V	Unequal phrase lengths Theme and variations

Alphabetical List of Songs

The letters in brackets refer to the acknowledgement of Sources (see p.224)

Sources

A *American Folk Songs for Children*, Ruth Crawford Seeger, Garden City, New York: Doubleday & Co., 1948

B *Baker's Dozen*, Jane Frazee and Arvida Steen, Minneapolis: Schmitt, Hall & McCreary (Now MGM), 1974

C *Echoes of Africa in Folk Songs of the Americas*, Beatrice Landeck, New York: Van Rees Press, 1961, 1969

D *Games & Songs of American Children*, William Wells Newell, New York: Dover Publications, 1963

E *Just Five*, Robert E. Kersey, New York: Belwin Mills, 1972

F *Just Five Plus Two*, Robert E. Kersey, New York: Belwin Mills, 1975

G *Music for Children* American Edition Vol.1: Schott Music Corp., 1982

H *Music for Children* American Edition Vol.2: Schott Music Corp., 1977

I *Music for Children* American Edition Vol.3: Schott Music Corp., 1980

J *Music for Children*, Margaret Murray, Vol.1: Schott & Co. Ltd., 1958

K *North Carolina Folklore*, Frank C. Brown Collection, Durham: Duke University Press

L *On the Trail of Negro Folk-Songs*, Dorothy Scarborough, Harboro, PA: Folklore Associates, 1963

M *Pentatonic Song Book*, Brian Brocklehurst, London: Schott & Co, 1968

N *Ring Around the Moon*, Edith Fowke, Englewood Cliffs, NJ: Prentice Hall Inc., 1977

O *Sally Go Round the Sun*, Edith Fowke, Garden City NY: Doubleday & Co., 1969

P *Seventeen Nursery Songs from the Appalachian Mountains*, Cecil Sharp, London: Novello

Q *Sing it Yourself*, Louise Larkins Bradford, Sherman Oaks, CA: Alfred Publishing Co., 1978

R *Songs of the Hill Folk*, J. J. Niles, New York: G. Schirmer, Inc., 1934

S *Ten Folk Carols*, Jane Frazee: Schott Music Corp., 1977

T *Wake Up and Sing!*, Beatrice Landeck and Elizabeth Crook, New York: Edward B. Marks, 1969

U *Windsongs, Method for the Recorder*, Birthe Kulich and Joe Berarducci, Vancouver: Empire Music, N.D.

We gratefully acknowledge the above sources of folk song material used in this book. Omission of any acknowledgement is regretted and will be corrected if brought to our attention. The source letter references appear in brackets beside the appropriate songs in the Alphabetical List of Songs (see p.223).